The Literature of Cinema

ADVISORY EDITOR: **MARTIN S. DWORKIN**
INSTITUTE OF PHILOSOPHY AND POLITICS OF EDUCATION
TEACHER'S COLLEGE, COLUMBIA UNIVERSITY

THE LITERATURE OF CINEMA presents
a comprehensive selection from the multitude
of writings about cinema, rediscovering materials on its origins, history, theoretical principles and techniques, aesthetics, economics,
and effects on societies and individuals. Included are works of inherent, lasting merit
and others of primarily historical significance.
These provide essential resources for serious
study and critical enjoyment of the "magic
shadows" that became one of the decisive cultural forces of modern times.

THE LITERATURE OF CINEMA presents a comprehensive selection from the multitude of writings about cinema, rediscovering materials on its origins, history, theoretical principles and techniques, aesthetics, economics, and effects on societies and individuals. Included are works of inherent, lasting merit and others of primarily historical significance. These provide essential resources for serious study and critical enjoyment of the "magic shadows" that became one of the decisive cultural forces of modern times.

Getting Ideas from the Movies

Perry W. Holaday and George D. Stoddard

ARNO PRESS & THE NEW YORK TIMES

New York • 1970

Reprint Edition 1970 by Arno Press Inc.
Library of Congress Catalog Card Number: 78-124029
ISBN 0-405-01647-6
ISBN for complete set: 0-405-01600-X
Manufactured in the United States of America

Getting Ideas from the Movies

Perry W. Holaday and George D. Stoddard

ARNO PRESS & THE NEW YORK TIMES

New York • 1970

Reprint Edition 1970 by Arno Press Inc.
Library of Congress Catalog Card Number: 78-124029
ISBN 0-405-01647-6
ISBN for complete set: 0-405-01600-X
Manufactured in the United States of America

Getting Ideas
from the Movies

Perry W. Holaday and George D. Stoddard

ARNO PRESS & THE NEW YORK TIMES

New York • 1970

Reprint Edition 1970 by Arno Press Inc.
Library of Congress Catalog Card Number: 78-124029
ISBN 0-405-01647-6
ISBN for complete set: 0-405-01600-X
Manufactured in the United States of America

GETTING IDEAS
FROM THE MOVIES

❖

PERRY W. HOLADAY
INDIANAPOLIS PUBLIC SCHOOLS

and

GEORGE D. STODDARD
DIRECTOR, IOWA CHILD WELFARE RESEARCH STATION,
THE STATE UNIVERSITY OF IOWA

NEW YORK
THE MACMILLAN COMPANY
1933

THIS SERIES OF TWELVE STUDIES OF THE
INFLUENCE OF MOTION PICTURES UPON
CHILDREN AND YOUTH HAS BEEN MADE BY
THE COMMITTEE ON EDUCATIONAL RE-
SEARCH OF THE PAYNE FUND AT THE RE-
QUEST OF THE NATIONAL COMMITTEE FOR
THE STUDY OF SOCIAL VALUES IN MOTION
PICTURES, NOW THE MOTION PICTURE RE-
SEARCH COUNCIL, 366 MADISON AVENUE,
NEW YORK CITY. THE STUDIES WERE DE-
SIGNED TO SECURE AUTHORITATIVE AND
IMPERSONAL DATA WHICH WOULD MAKE
POSSIBLE A MORE COMPLETE EVALUATION
OF MOTION PICTURES AND THEIR SOCIAL
POTENTIALITIES

ACKNOWLEDGMENTS

Dr. W. W. Charters of Ohio State University, director of the series of motion picture experiments of which this is one, has greatly facilitated the organization and accomplishment of the later portion of the study. Mrs. Elva Porter and others were of considerable assistance in the construction, administration, and evaluation of tests. The Ohio Censorship Board and the Columbus, Ohio, representatives of two motion picture corporations are to be thanked for the previews of pictures. Lastly, the authors wish to express their appreciation to the several thousand observers who entered so whole-heartedly into the experiment.

TABLE OF CONTENTS

LIST OF TABLES

GETTING IDEAS FROM THE MOVIES

CHAPTER I

ORGANIZATION OF THE INVESTIGATION

A description of the aims of the study.—This investigation is an attempt to measure two effects of motion pictures on the memories of children: the retention of film content and the changes in quantity and accuracy of general information, including the direction and duration of the changes. What scenes in a picture stay best in a child's memory? To what degree are geography, history, and other information subjects incidentally taught by pictures created primarily for entertainment? These effects were studied by testing children on the content of selected motion pictures to which they had been sent.

The original impetus.—This study was one of a group of studies made for the purpose of investigating the effect of motion pictures on children.[1] The problem was subdivided into several parts, and each was placed in the hands of a research expert who was allotted sufficient funds to develop his particular division according to an outline which he had previously prepared. The method of investigation for this portion of the problem was originally outlined by George D. Stoddard, and the preliminary steps of the experiment were organized around his outline. As originally planned, the study consisted of an investigation into the amounts and

[1] This series is entitled "Motion Pictures and Youth." The studies reported are listed on page ii of this volume.

kinds of general information gained and the retention of specific incidents in the pictures, together with the duration of the retention of both types of information. Later, it was found possible to carry on related investigations with profit to the study and without interfering with the essential data. Since the field of investigation covered by this report was large, emphasis was placed on an analysis of tendencies rather than on a final settlement of any single portion of the problem.

More than 3,000 observers took one or more tests. There were 17 pictures and 26 tests consisting of from 30 to 64 items each, aggregating more than 20,000 testings with approximately 813,000 items attempted.

Preliminary steps in the investigation.—The first steps consisted in the development of techniques for picture analysis and test construction. Preliminary analyses were made of 17 pictures. These were written in story form, but the principal factor in each analysis was the determination of the testing possibilities of the picture. Analyses of pictures were made on two other occasions during the study. These picture analyses served three purposes: they showed whether or not the pictures were adapted to the conditions and purposes of the study; they were useful for practice in preparing questions about the different types of action shown; and they aided in the general classification of pictures according to types (emotional, humorous, and the like) and according to use in testing.

As a further preliminary step in the experiment, two pictures, "The Gaucho" and "The Baby Cyclone," were selected for experimental analysis and test construction. Each picture was analyzed by a number of persons who were expert in dramatics, in art and architecture, or in domestic science, as well as by a stenographer and by one of the investigators. Each observed items which fell within his field. The dramatic critic wrote characterizations of the principal actors, in which he mentioned as many illustrations from the picture as possible. The art teacher and the domestic-science expert gave descriptions of clothing, furnishings, and modes of transportation. The stenographer wrote a brief summary of the plot and copied the titles and subheadings. The investigator listed items of historical, geographical, scientific, or general interest which might have been missed by the others.

From the material produced by these analyses, tests of the type used in the first three pictures were carried far enough to insure the value of the technique employed. These tests were not completed because they were not to be used; they were for practice only. They showed, however, that it was possible to construct tests which would measure adequately the main factual items of a picture. This plan for the construction of tests was continued with minor variations throughout the experiment. In September, 1929, another picture, "The Dance of Life," was similarly analyzed, and a few trial questions formulated.

Tests for the first picture.—The observation of the first picture used in the experiment, "Sorrell and Son," was carried out as just described. A complete analysis of the picture was prepared as a basis for the construction of two tests, one of general and one of specific information. The general-information test consisted of 25 yes-no items and 10 multiple-choice items, covering the customs, history, and life in England during the period shown in the picture. All questions could be answered after seeing the picture if they were not known previously, but any of them could have been answered by a well-informed individual who had not seen the picture. Examples of these questions are:

Yes-no test—

————Are there large hotels anywhere except in America? ("Sorrell and Son," General, Part 1, No. 15.) The directions for this test ask the subject to write "yes" or "no" in front of each question according to the truth or falsity of the item. Multiple-choice test—

A famous English University is 1. Yale, 2. Harvard, 3. Princeton, 4. Oxford. ("Sorrell and Son," General, Part 2, No. 3.) The directions ask the subject to underline the correct response.[2]

The percentages of correct responses [3] on each item for each age-group on each testing showed definitely that certain changes in mental content had taken place as a result of seeing the picture. The various testings for the general-information test [4] of "Sorrell and Son" were:

Pretest—the general-information test administered before seeing the picture.

General—the same test administered to the same groups the day after the picture.

One-Month General (1 General)—the same test administered a month after the picture.

If item No. 15, Part 1, of the general-information test for "Sorrell and Son" is considered in terms of percentages of correct responses by each age-group on each testing, the following data are obtained:

[2] A very much better technique was used in later testing, as illustrated in the following question:

"A man who tried to conquer Russia and failed was   (1) Charlemagne   (2) Napoleon   (3) Achilles   (4) Wellington   (5) Mussolini.
         1( )   2( )   3( )   4( )   5( )
("New Moon," General, No. 17.) The directions ask that a cross be placed in the parentheses with the same number as the correct answer. Scoring was done with a stencil laid over the test so that the correct and incorrect answers could be quickly detected and tabulated.

[3] Every effort was made to obtain the correct answer to each question; that is, the answer generally accepted by the leading authorities. In analyses of answers, the percentages of correct (accepted) answers of the entire age-group on each item were the criteria used in the evaluation of data rather than total scores of individuals within the group.

[4] Throughout the tables in this study, these designations are usually represented by the terms Pretest, General, and 1 General, respectively.

Age-Group	PERCENTAGES OF CORRECT RESPONSES		
	Pretest	General	1 General
Second-third grade................	10	50	84
Fifth-sixth grade..................	48	70	76
Ninth-tenth grade.................	86	100	100
Adults...........................	92	96	100

There are minor eccentricities in the data, but it is noticeable that each group gained in the average amount of general information concerning this item. The Pretest was given the morning of the day the picture was seen, and the General test was given the following morning. In this interval of one day the movie was the only known variation from everyday experience. Since a similar change was found in practically every correctly shown item used in the tests, the pictures can probably be held accountable for the changes in general information. Although the item described is of minor importance, the sum total of similar items covers an important sector of human knowledge. The percentages in such tables indicate the amount of general information gained from pictures as a whole since the pictures used in the experiment constituted an adequate cross section of motion pictures.

There is frequently a maturation effect shown in these tests. As in the case of the item quoted, the memory of the picture and the utilization of the general information gained from it are occasionally better over a longer period of time than over a shorter. In this case the percentages of correct responses were higher a month after the picture than they were the day after.

The age-groups [5] used as observers in this experiment consisted of the following:

[5] The terms "second-third," "fifth-sixth," "ninth-tenth," and "adults" will be used to designate the particular section of each age-group given the test. In the various tables, the designations here given are further abbreviated to 2-3, 5-6, and 9-10.

Second-third—all available children in the second and third
  grades of the schools tested.
Fifth-sixth—all available children in the fifth and sixth grades
  of these schools.
Ninth-tenth—all available children in the ninth and tenth
  grades of these schools.
Adults—groups of 75 and 125 superior adults.

For each subsequent picture, with one exception, a test of
specific information covering the action, background, and
characterization of the movie was constructed. The specific-
information tests for "Sorrell and Son" were given twice:

Specific—the specific-information test given the day following
  the picture.
One-Month Specific (1 Specific)—the same test administered to
  the same groups a month after the picture.

All tests mentioned in this report, both general- and
specific-information tests, are referred to by the designations
mentioned. [6] In each case, the name of the picture for which
the test was constructed is appended unless it is clearly
understood. The "Mysterious Island" Specific or the
"Moran of the Marines" One-Month General will be understood as the specific-information test for "Mysterious
Island" taken the day after the picture and of the general-
information test for "Moran of the Marines" taken one
month after the picture was seen. Any time element mentioned in the description of the test refers to the length of
time intervening between the picture and the administration
of the test. During the last year of the experiment the One-
Month General (1 General) and the One-Month Specific
(1 Specific) tests were replaced by the One-and-a-Half-
Month General (1½ General) and Specific (1½ Specific),
and a Three-Month Specific (3 Specific) was added. For
one picture a Seven-Month Specific (7 Specific) was used.

[6] *See* footnote 4, page 4.

Tests for the first three pictures consisted of yes-no and four-response multiple-choice items. For the pictures of the following year the yes-no items were replaced by completion items, and the four-response multiple-choice items were replaced by those of the five-response type. An example of the completion tests used follows:

> Three days later he received word that his terms were accepted, and he started to go to ————. ("General Crack," Specific, Part 1, No. 14)

Directions ask that the word necessary to complete the meaning be written in the blank. This type of testing was used for specific-information tests only. Evaluation of the efficiency of these techniques and of various additions made to the testing program will be found in the next chapter.

The 17 pictures used in the experiment were:

1928-30:

"Sorrell and Son"—Drama of war-time and postwar England. Silent.

"Moran of the Marines"—Humorous treatment of life in the marine corps at home and abroad. Silent.

"The Midnight Taxi"—Light drama of crook life. Talking sequences.

"Kitty"—Romantic drama of postwar England. Talking sequences.

"Why Bring That Up?"—Humorous account of the rise to fame of the Two Black Crows of phonograph fame. All talking.

"The Four Feathers"—War in the Sudan and life in England. Very good shots of native and animal life. Silent.

"Mysterious Island"—Melodramatic phantasy of life in an undersea kingdom. Technicolor. Talking sequences.

"Return of Sherlock Holmes"—The mysterious adventures of the famous detective. All talking.

"Show of Shows"—A revue carried out in motion pictures. A number of scenes exploiting motion-picture stars. Mostly technicolor. All talking.

"General Crack"—Romantic drama of war and love in Austria of 1740. All talking.

1930–31: [7]

"Tom Sawyer"—The adventures of Mark Twain's boy hero and his friends.

"Passion Flower"—A drama of modern society, based upon the familiar triangle plot.

"Gang Buster"—A comedy of crooks and their actions.

"New Moon"—Musical romance of love and fighting at a frontier fort in pre-war Russia.

"Fighting Caravans"—Stirring melodrama of life in a wagon train crossing the plains in the early 1860's.

"Stolen Heaven"—Drama of Palm Beach society life.

"Rango"—Native and animal life in Sumatra. This picture is quite scenic but contains a record rather than a story. No test of specific information was used.

Summary.—This study was planned to determine the amounts of general information retained by children after viewing a motion picture and the specific incidents of the picture remembered by them over brief and long periods of time. The subjects consisted of approximately 3,000 children in the second, third, fifth, sixth, ninth, and tenth grades and 200 superior adults. All were sent to 17 motion pictures upon which they were tested. Each general-information test covered general items of information shown in the picture and was administered as a pretest the day before the picture and again the day following the picture and a month later. Each specific-information test covered the action, background, and characterization of a particular picture and was administered the day following the picture and again a month later. Certain variations in the time of testing were introduced in the last year of study.

[7] Pictures used during these years were all talking.

CHAPTER II

TECHNIQUES USED IN THE STUDY

Combinations of test data.—This experiment was based partially upon the assumption that a carefully selected group of motion pictures, embracing all current types, would constitute a fair sampling of motion pictures as a whole. This assumption was later proved empirically. If the study is so constructed that it has for a basis a cross section of the totality of motion pictures for the years 1928–30, a closer scrutiny of this cross section is in order.

A motion picture is not an entire unit by itself. A humorous picture is not entirely humorous to the exclusion of other types of material; it is simply a picture in which the element of humor predominates although other elements are present in varying and unpredictable amounts. A direct comparison upon any basis of two humorous pictures is not feasible because of this factor, for the other elements are not necessarily similar for the two pictures and may cause an unpredictable effect upon any comparisons of the total pictures. In a sense, the humorous elements of two pictures are themselves not comparable, but a comparison of these partials is a more logical step than comparisons of total pictures. If, however, the group of pictures selected for the study is described as a cross section of pictures as a whole, the situation changes. The pictures are considered as a group and assume a more unitary aspect. There is no longer any motive for comparing humorous items from picture to picture, since the entire group of humorous items from all of the pictures also assumes a unitary aspect. Comparisons are now to be found between the sum total of humorous items and the sum total of items of other types. This comparison is based upon items drawn from all pictures in the study, rather than from one alone.

For this reason the total scores of individuals on motion-picture tests are considered less important than average scores of the various age-groups on particular test items. Individual scores are based upon entire but single pictures, whereas individual items can be grouped according to definite types. This permits really important comparisons to be made throughout the entire group of pictures.

Equation of groups of observers.—During the first year and a half the study was conducted at the University of Iowa. The three youngest groups of observers were taken largely from the elementary school and the high school conducted by the University. The adults consisted largely of graduate students in the University and their wives. Some students from the Training School of Iowa State Teachers College observed several pictures and answered the tests. Pretests of "Moran of the Marines" and "The Midnight Taxi" were also given at Washington, Iowa, and Cedar Rapids, Iowa.

During the last year the experiment was conducted at Ohio State University, Columbus, Ohio. This move was taken for three reasons: First, since Columbus is the capital of Ohio, the Ohio State Division of Film Censorship is located there, and previews of pictures could be obtained at the office of the State Division or at the local district offices of two motion-picture concerns considerably in advance of the actual exhibition of the pictures. Second, it was possible at Columbus to obtain larger groups of observers who came from more varied types of communities than could be found in Iowa. Third, while obtaining the two first-named advan-

TABLE I (*Continued*)

AVERAGE AGES, READING AGES, MENTAL AGES, AND INTELLIGENCE QUOTIENTS FOR ALL GROUPS (*Continued*)

	GRADES 2–3	GRADES 5–6	GRADES 9–10	ADULTS
	Data from the 1930–31 Study [a]			
	Chronological Ages			
Jackson:				
A	6–11	10– 4	14– 7	......
B	6– 8	10– 2	14– 7	......
C	7– 1	10– 6	14– 7	......
Columbus:				
A	8– 2	10–11	15– 2	28–9
B	8– 9	11– 0	15– 1	29–5
C	8– 2	11– 4	14– 7	28–6
Delaware:				
A	7– 8	10– 6	14–10	......
B	6– 8	9– 9	14–10	......
C	6– 6	10– 9	15– 2	......
Wellsburg:				
A	8– 4	11– 8	15– 4	......
B	8– 8	11– 6	15– 2	......
C	8– 8	11– 3	15– 3	......
Avondale and Walnut Hills:				
A	7–10	10–10	14– 1	......
B	7–10	10– 9	14– 1	......
C	7–11	10–10	14– 0	......
Raschig and Woodward:				
A	7–10	12– 8	......	......
B	8–10	12– 2	......	......
C	8–10	12– 4	......	......
	Mental Ages			
Columbus:				
A	8– 1	......	14–11	......
B	7– 7	......	14–11	......
C	7– 9	......	14–10	......
Avondale:				
A	......	11–4	......	......
B	......	11–1	......	......
C	......	11–3	......	......
	Scores on Stanford Reading			
Jackson:				
A	59	158	207	......
B	58	161	194	......
C	59	159	206	......

[a] All existing data are included. Blanks indicate that information is not available for that group.

TABLE I (*Continued*)

AVERAGE AGES, READING AGES, MENTAL AGES, AND
INTELLIGENCE QUOTIENTS FOR ALL GROUPS (*Continued*)

	GRADES 2–3	GRADES 5–6	GRADES 9–10	ADULTS
	Scores on Stanford Achievement Test			
Raschig:				
A........................	32	71	......	....
B........................	32	71	......	....
C........................	33	70	......	....
	Intelligence Quotients			
Columbus:				
A........................	101	......	99	....
B........................	95	......	100	....
C........................	97	......	102	....
Avondale:				
A........................	......	104	......	....
B........................	......	107	......	....
C........................	......	105	......	....
Woodward:				
A...:....................	......	......	102	....
B........................	......	......	101	....
C........................	......	......	101	....
	Scores on Otis Group Intelligence Scale [d]			
Jackson:				
A........................	45.9	......	......	....
B........................	46.2	......	......	....
C........................	47.3	......	......	....
	Scores on Otis Self-Administering Test [e]			
Jackson:				
A........................	......	43.0	45.9	59.3
B........................	......	44.8	46.3	56.5
C........................	......	43.3	45.8	60.3
	Scores on Terman Group Test			
Wellsburg:				
A........................	......	......	121.7	....
B........................	...:..	......	120.8	....
C........................	......	......	115.8	....

[d] Primary.
[e] Intermediate and higher.

relationship between ability to answer a test on a movie and to write a theme about it. Correlations between the number of facts given in themes and the scores on General or Specific tests for "Sorrell and Son" were low but positive. The themes varied from the following contribution in the second grade, "it was interesting, i thought," to the polished, typed synopses written by graduate students. The total number of facts from each age-group were classified according to seventeen categories—the thirteen scenes of the picture, the names of characters, comments on the picture, mistakes, and items which could not be classified in one of the other groups. Responses varied considerably, for observers in each age-group commented on what to them seemed to be the most pertinent items. Mistakes in fact were far more common for younger children than for adults. Statistical treatment was impossible with these data.

One further attempt at the theme technique was made during the testing of the picture "Kitty." Adult observers were asked to describe the relations existing between Kitty and her mother-in-law. Possibly, because of the limited range of the topic or the subjective type of topic, the themes were even more difficult to analyze than were those for "Sorrell and Son," and the attempt to adapt this type of questioning to the uses of the study was abandoned.

The true-false type of item is not thoroughly usable for research of this type. In theory, correction for guessing makes the true-false item a valid type to use; and where the main point of interest is the obtaining of the relative standings of various individuals in an academic course, the true-false question is satisfactory. In this study, the main emphasis is not upon individual scores, which are practically disregarded, but upon percentages of correct responses upon each item. When a test of general information is given as a pretest preceding the picture for which it was constructed, the true-false type of question might yield satisfactory results; when the same test is administered to groups which have seen the picture, however, many of the effects of the picture upon the observers are lost in the corrections for chance usually in use with true-false questions. Consider for an instant a hypothetical test item. If the tests for "The Mysterious Island," a movie containing many contrary-to-fact situations, had been constructed partly or entirely of the yes-no type, one question might have been worded: "Can a submarine receive radio messages while it is 100 feet deep under the water?" According to physics this is an impossibility,[2] yet the action is shown in the picture. In an adult group which had seen the picture, there might be 40 per cent who were certain of the facts of the case and still responded "no" regardless of the action shown on the screen, while an additional 20 per cent were uncertain and half answered "yes" and half "no," and the remaining 40 per cent accepted the movie as an authority and answered "yes." The answers of the ones who really knew the accepted answer would be lost as the percentage of correct responses would be 50 per cent minus 50 per cent or zero, whereas there were 40 per cent of the group really conversant with the true facts of the case. This is an exaggerated, but perfectly possible, situation. Another item might receive a much larger percentage of correct answers than it deserves because of its wording. If a question had been asked in this same test: "Was the first successful submarine built by the English?" the correct answer would be "no," as the honor is usually ascribed to Robert Fulton, an American, who constructed a ship of this type for the French government.

[2] Morecroft, J. D., *Principles of Radio Communication*, 2d ed., London, John Wiley and Sons, 1927, p. 843.

relationship between ability to answer a test on a movie and to write a theme about it. Correlations between the number of facts given in themes and the scores on General or Specific tests for "Sorrell and Son" were low but positive. The themes varied from the following contribution in the second grade, "it was interesting, i thought," to the polished, typed synopses written by graduate students. The total number of facts from each age-group were classified according to seventeen categories—the thirteen scenes of the picture, the names of characters, comments on the picture, mistakes, and items which could not be classified in one of the other groups. Responses varied considerably, for observers in each age-group commented on what to them seemed to be the most pertinent items. Mistakes in fact were far more common for younger children than for adults. Statistical treatment was impossible with these data.

One further attempt at the theme technique was made during the testing of the picture "Kitty." Adult observers were asked to describe the relations existing between Kitty and her mother-in-law. Possibly, because of the limited range of the topic or the subjective type of topic, the themes were even more difficult to analyze than were those for "Sorrell and Son," and the attempt to adapt this type of questioning to the uses of the study was abandoned.

The true-false type of item is not thoroughly usable for research of this type. In theory, correction for guessing makes the true-false item a valid type to use; and where the main point of interest is the obtaining of the relative standings of various individuals in an academic course, the true-false question is satisfactory. In this study, the main emphasis is not upon individual scores, which are practically disregarded, but upon percentages of correct responses upon each item. When a test of general information is given as a pretest preceding the picture for which it was constructed, the true-false type of question might yield satisfactory results; when the same test is administered to groups which have seen the picture, however, many of the effects of the picture upon the observers are lost in the corrections for chance usually in use with true-false questions. Consider for an instant a hypothetical test item. If the tests for "The Mysterious Island," a movie containing many contrary-to-fact situations, had been constructed partly or entirely of the yes-no type, one question might have been worded: "Can a submarine receive radio messages while it is 100 feet deep under the water?" According to physics this is an impossibility,[2] yet the action is shown in the picture. In an adult group which had seen the picture, there might be 40 per cent who were certain of the facts of the case and still responded "no" regardless of the action shown on the screen, while an additional 20 per cent were uncertain and half answered "yes" and half "no," and the remaining 40 per cent accepted the movie as an authority and answered "yes." The answers of the ones who really knew the accepted answer would be lost as the percentage of correct responses would be 50 per cent minus 50 per cent or zero, whereas there were 40 per cent of the group really conversant with the true facts of the case. This is an exaggerated, but perfectly possible, situation. Another item might receive a much larger percentage of correct answers than it deserves because of its wording. If a question had been asked in this same test: "Was the first successful submarine built by the English?" the correct answer would be "no," as the honor is usually ascribed to Robert Fulton, an American, who constructed a ship of this type for the French government.

[2] Morecroft, J. D., *Principles of Radio Communication*, 2d ed., London, John Wiley and Sons, 1927, p. 843.

8. Drinking—In those days, the people of Austria drank principally (1) water (2) coffee (3) wine (4) tea (5) whiskey ("General Crack," General No. 10).
9. General Conversation—The Duke said that the sound of cannon made him (1) angry (2) afraid (3) sad (4) homesick (5) happy ("General Crack," Part 2, No. 2).
—This movie was made by (1) Metro-Goldwyn (2) Fox (3) Warner Bros. (4) Universal (5) Paramount ("Why Bring That Up?" Part 1, No. 2).
10. General Action—Frank Fay announced the next act. He was dressed in a soldier's uniform and wore a number of medals ("Show of Shows," No. 6).

In classifying items, the reference is not to the question itself, but to the action carried on in the particular portion of the picture covered by the question. For example in the item

When Moran was talking to Betty about the jewelry he had bought her, he called it (1) ice (2) fruit (3) liquid fire (4) glass (5) cards ("Why Bring That Up?" Part 1, No. 23).

there is apparently nothing but general conversation, yet the movie at this point shows a man who is desperate because he realizes that the girl he loves has been playing with him, has influenced him to steal from his partner, has caused injury and possible death to his partner. The question is therefore classified as emotional. All items given as illustrations are quite clear-cut as to type, and there are many others that can be classified with similar ease. However, in the case of certain questions the classifications necessarily rest upon the judgments of three persons who saw the movies many times and, with the aid of others, constructed the tests. The judgments were admittedly subjective. Definite instructions for classifying the items were formulated and followed by the three observers, and all the judgments were agreed to by all observers. The sectioning of items rested probably upon the expert opinion available at the time.

Three methods were used in correlating the items from the 1929–30 tests and the content of selected films. All three experiments tried showed high relationship between the percentages of the various kinds of action found in test items and in movies in general. This classification will again be referred to in connection with the analysis of results. The classifications used in this section are not intended to be all-inclusive, but simply to cover all the action of the pictures used.

As a further check on the validity of the testing, a number of children and adults were given both the oral and the usual mimeographed test for "Stolen Heaven." Oral testing was done individually and preceded the written test. The examiner was provided with a list of the 40 questions included in the mimeographed Specific test. The subject was asked to tell the story of the picture. Each question of those in the test answered voluntarily, whether correctly or incorrectly, was so checked by the examiner. After the story had been told, the examiner went back over the test and asked the questions which had been omitted, using a standardized wording for each question. No list of possible solutions was presented; the questions were entirely of the recall type. After all children included in the experiment had been thus tested, all were given the regular mimeographed Specific test. This procedure was followed for 34 children from Avondale and Woodward High School at Cincinnati and 17 adults, 30 children from the Bureau of Juvenile Research at Columbus (Specific), and 23 children from Heyl and South High at Columbus (1½ Specific). The data from this experiment as given in Table III definitely show that the questions constructed to cover the picture are the ones answered in the telling of the story of the picture. Reliabilities are not furnished for the third group, the 1½ Specific for Columbus, as only a few children were available at each age-level.

In the case of the students tested on the oral test for "Stolen Heaven," the children from the best district at Cincinnati had average scores on both oral and written tests lower than those of the corresponding groups from the Bureau of Juvenile Research. The children in this institution are committed there as being either disciplinary or social-problem cases, and they live under the constant restriction of an institution. They saw the picture under less favorable conditions, and they were less familiar with the methods used in testing. In addition to having higher scores than the public-school children, they had reliabilities nearly as high, and for two out of three age-groups, there was a higher percentage on the oral tests as compared to the written.

This experiment showed several things: First, there was a high relationship between actual retention of the picture and scores on formal written tests. Second, the scores on oral tests were approximately 85 per cent as high as scores on written tests. Third, the findings of this study apply to all types of subjects. When the proper stimuli (the mimeographed tests used in this study) are applied, the details and action of a picture can be recalled with a high degree of accuracy, regardless of the make-up of the group of subjects. Finally, these tests cover quite accurately the material of the picture. The validity of the tests is satisfactory if the following facts are kept in mind: (1) the tests possessed sufficient range to accommodate both second-grade children and university graduates; (2) there was no opportunity for revision or standardization as tests were used as soon as constructed; (3) the tests were short, being only 40 to 60 questions long, on account of the length of school time available for their administration.

TABLE III

A COMPARISON OF AVERAGE PERCENTAGES OF CORRECT
RESPONSES ON ORAL AND WRITTEN SPECIFIC TESTS
FOR "STOLEN HEAVEN"

Group	Type of Test	Grades 2–3	Grades 5–6	Grades 9–10	Adults
Oral test:					
Cincinnati................	Specific	44.4	69.3	78.4	74.6
Bureau of Juvenile Research................	Specific	52.9	73.9	83.1	....
Columbus................	1½ Specific	40.0	53.8	63.1	....
Written test:					
Cincinnati................	Specific	62.1	76.6	84.8	80.9
Bureau of Juvenile Research................	Specific	63.7	79.9	86.3	....
Columbus................	1½ Specific	49.3	66.3	68.8	....
Percentage oral is of written:					
Cincinnati................	Specific	71.5	90.5	92.5	92.2
Bureau of Juvenile Research................	Specific	83.0	72.5	96.3	....
Columbus................	1½ Specific	81.1	81.1	91.7	....
	Measures of Reliability of Test				
Oral test:					
Cincinnati................	Specific	.69	.56	.29	.90
Bureau of Juvenile Research................	Specific	.53	.74	.83	....
Written test:					
Cincinnati................	Specific	.85	.85	.82	.70
Bureau of Juvenile Research................	Specific	.64	.80	.86	....
Correlation of oral with written:					
Cincinnati	Specific	.92	.73	.66	.84
Bureau of Juvenile Research................	Specific	.82	.78	.88	....

This table should be read as follows: Children in the second-third grade-
group at Cincinnati answered 44.4 per cent of the questions on the oral test
and 62.1 per cent of the questions on the written test, or they were 71.5 per
cent as high on the oral as on the written test, and so on. The reliabilities of
the oral tests are not so high as those of the written tests, but the correlations
between scores on oral and written tests are quite high.

Reliability of tests.—The reliabilities of these tests are shown in Table IV. The reliabilities are higher for tests of the later pictures than for tests used for the first three pictures of the study, due partly at least to improvements in test construction. These tests were shorter for the second-third group than for the others during the 1929–30 portion of the study and possibly more difficult of comprehension. The reliabilities for this group therefore fluctuate from testing to testing more than do those of the other age-groups. All reliabilities for tests were obtained by correlating the odd- and even-numbered items and stepping up the obtained value by means of the Spearman-Brown prophecy formula. The factors which were mentioned as influencing the validity of the tests also affected their reliability, and in the light of this fact the reliabilities obtained are superior to what might have been expected in a study of this type.

Relationships existing between Specific and General tests.— At four points of the study, groups took the General and the Specific tests the same day. The correlations between the scores made on the two tests are high. Frequently, the correlation between the two tests is higher than the reliability of one of the tests, and in one instance it is greater than the reliability of either test. There is a definite relationship shown between the contents of the two types of tests since correlations between them are so uniform and are fairly high. Many of the items which were used for test construction could have been made into either general or specific test items.

Relationships between scores on motion-picture tests and age, mental age, reading age, and educational age.—At various times during the progress of the study, correlations were obtained between the scores on motion-picture tests and age, mental age, educational age, or reading age, which were

TABLE IV

RELIABILITIES OF TESTS USED IN THIS EXPERIMENT DURING 1929–31

TYPE OF TEST	GRADES 2–3		GRADES 5–6		GRADES 9–10		ADULT	
	Range	Median	Range	Median	Range	Median	Range	Median
General information:								
Pretest............	.36–67	.56	.32–80	.60	.47–.78	.60	.46–85	.62
General............	.10–83	.75	.60–79	.64	.65–89	.70	.49–82	.69
1 and 1½ General...	.41–78	.66	.50–89	.75	.65–89	.75	.60–80	.68
2 General..........	.70–91	.90	.....	.....	.....	.....	.....	.....
Specific information:								
Specific...........	.50–89	.75	.79–95	.87	.77–.95	.84	.56–97	.72
1 and 1½ Specific..	.21–85	.70	.73–91	.85	.63–96	.85	.66–97	.85
2 and 3 Specific...	.54–94	.76	.77–91	.87	.77–87	.82	.62–91	.87

This table should be read as follows: Reliabilities on tests of general information given to the second-third grade-group before seeing the pictures (Pretests) ranged from .36 to .67 with a median of .56, whereas the reliabilities of the same tests given to this age-group after seeing the pictures ranged from .10 to .83, the median being higher than the highest reliability made on the Pretests, and so on. The reliabilities of general-information tests were higher for groups which had seen the pictures than for groups which had not. Tests of specific information were more reliable than tests of general information.

Reliability of tests.—The reliabilities of these tests are shown in Table IV. The reliabilities are higher for tests of the later pictures than for tests used for the first three pictures of the study, due partly at least to improvements in test construction. These tests were shorter for the second-third group than for the others during the 1929–30 portion of the study and possibly more difficult of comprehension. The reliabilities for this group therefore fluctuate from testing to testing more than do those of the other age-groups. All reliabilities for tests were obtained by correlating the odd- and even-numbered items and stepping up the obtained value by means of the Spearman-Brown prophecy formula. The factors which were mentioned as influencing the validity of the tests also affected their reliability, and in the light of this fact the reliabilities obtained are superior to what might have been expected in a study of this type.

Relationships existing between Specific and General tests.— At four points of the study, groups took the General and the Specific tests the same day. The correlations between the scores made on the two tests are high. Frequently, the correlation between the two tests is higher than the reliability of one of the tests, and in one instance it is greater than the reliability of either test. There is a definite relationship shown between the contents of the two types of tests since correlations between them are so uniform and are fairly high. Many of the items which were used for test construction could have been made into either general or specific test items.

Relationships between scores on motion-picture tests and age, mental age, reading age, and educational age.—At various times during the progress of the study, correlations were obtained between the scores on motion-picture tests and age, mental age, educational age, or reading age, which were

TABLE IV

RELIABILITIES OF TESTS USED IN THIS EXPERIMENT DURING 1929-31

TYPE OF TEST	GRADES 2-3		GRADES 5-6		GRADES 9-10		ADULT	
	Range	Median	Range	Median	Range	Median	Range	Median
General information:								
Pretest	.36-67	.56	.32-.80	.60	.47-78	.60	.46-.85	.62
General	.10-83	.75	.60-.79	.64	.65-.89	.70	.49-.82	.69
1 and 1½ General	.41-78	.66	.50-.89	.75	.65-.89	.75	.60-.80	.68
2 General	.70-91	.90	......	......	......	......	......	......
Specific information:								
Specific	.50-.89	.75	.79-.95	.87	.77-.95	.84	.56-.97	.72
1 and 1½ Specific	.21-.85	.70	.73-.91	.85	.63-.96	.85	.66-.97	.85
2 and 3 Specific	.54-.94	.76	.77-.91	.87	.77-.87	.82	.62-.91	.87

This table should be read as follows: Reliabilities on tests of general information given to the second-third grade-group before seeing the pictures (Pretests) ranged from .36 to .67 with a median of .56, whereas the reliabilities of the same tests given to this age-group after seeing the pictures ranged from .10 to .83, the median being higher than the highest reliability made on the Pretests, and so on. The reliabilities of general-information tests were higher for groups which had seen the pictures than for groups which had not. Tests of specific information were more reliable than tests of general information.

Reliability of tests.—The reliabilities of these tests are shown in Table IV. The reliabilities are higher for tests of the later pictures than for tests used for the first three pictures of the study, due partly at least to improvements in test construction. These tests were shorter for the second-third group than for the others during the 1929–30 portion of the study and possibly more difficult of comprehension. The reliabilities for this group therefore fluctuate from testing to testing more than do those of the other age-groups. All reliabilities for tests were obtained by correlating the odd- and even-numbered items and stepping up the obtained value by means of the Spearman-Brown prophecy formula. The factors which were mentioned as influencing the validity of the tests also affected their reliability, and in the light of this fact the reliabilities obtained are superior to what might have been expected in a study of this type.

Relationships existing between Specific and General tests.—At four points of the study, groups took the General and the Specific tests the same day. The correlations between the scores made on the two tests are high. Frequently, the correlation between the two tests is higher than the reliability of one of the tests, and in one instance it is greater than the reliability of either test. There is a definite relationship shown between the contents of the two types of tests since correlations between them are so uniform and are fairly high. Many of the items which were used for test construction could have been made into either general or specific test items.

Relationships between scores on motion-picture tests and age, mental age, reading age, and educational age.—At various times during the progress of the study, correlations were obtained between the scores on motion-picture tests and age, mental age, educational age, or reading age, which were

TABLE IV

RELIABILITIES OF TESTS USED IN THIS EXPERIMENT DURING 1929-31

TYPE OF TEST	GRADES 2-3		GRADES 5-6		GRADES 9-10		ADULT	
	Range	Median	Range	Median	Range	Median	Range	Median
General information:								
Pretest..........	.36-.67	.56	.32-.80	.60	.47-.78	.60	.46-.85	.62
General..........	.10-.83	.75	.60-.79	.64	.65-.89	.70	.49-.82	.69
1 and 1½ General....	.41-.78	.66	.50-.89	.75	.65-.89	.75	.60-.80	.68
2 General.........	.70-.91	.90	.....	.....	.....	.....	.....	.....
Specific information:								
Specific..........	.50-.89	.75	.79-.95	.87	.77-.95	.84	.56-.97	.72
1 and 1½ Specific.....	.21-.85	.70	.73-.91	.85	.63-.96	.85	.66-.97	.85
2 and 3 Specific......	.54-.94	.76	.77-.91	.87	.77-.87	.82	.62-.91	.87

This table should be read as follows: Reliabilities on tests of general information given to the second-third grade-group before seeing the pictures (Pretests) ranged from .36 to .67 with a median of .56, whereas the reliabilities of the same tests given to this age-group after seeing the pictures ranged from .10 to .83, the median being higher than the highest reliability made on the Pretests, and so on. The reliabilities of general-information tests were higher for groups which had seen the pictures than for groups which had not. Tests of specific information were more reliable than tests of general information.

obtained for the most part from school records. These correlations, of which more than 100 were computed, were quite low. Only two were more than .80, and most of them were but little above 0. In almost every case the correlation between a motion-picture test and age, mental age, or other measure was less than the reliability of the test. Jones found a high relationship between scores on tests of this type and Army Alpha, but his groups consisted of observers ranging in age from ten years to more than forty.[5] This range of talent would naturally cause a higher correlation between the two measures than would be the case if his group had been sectioned into two or three subgroups according to age, and these subgroups had been measured separately. The ability to remember the salient facts of a motion picture is a trait somewhat related to mental ability, reading ability, or general ability to learn, but the relationship is not strong.

Sectioning of questions according to kinds of action, types of action, and background.—The sectioning of this type which was carried out in 1929–30 has been described. During 1930–31, further refinements were effected. The 240 questions in the 6 tests of specific information were classified according to 10 kinds of action which occurred. These classifications were carefully defined beforehand, but definitions and examples of each kind of action were rather lengthy and will not be included. The kinds of action occurring in these pictures were emotion, crime, drinking, fighting, mystery, romance, sports, social activities, general conversation, and general action. The 7 types of action shown in these pictures were humorous, romantic, sad, strongly emotional, weakly emotional, neutral, and titles. The 12 kinds of background in which the action occurred were business, café, frontier,

---

[5] Conrad, Herbert S., and Jones, Harold Ellis, *Psychological Studies of Motion Pictures. III. Fidelity of Report as a Measure of Adult Intelligence.* University of California Publications in Psychology, 1918–1929 (1929, No. 7), 3, 245–276.

hotel, home, war, tenement, school, seas and ships, general exterior, outdoors, and titles.

Summary.—The group of motion pictures used in this experiment is considered a cross section of all pictures, this unitary aspect making it possible to combine the test data on all items of the same general type occurring in the various pictures. In each locality, each age-group was divided into three sections, equated on the basis of chronological age, mental age, and reading age. Each of the three administrations of each test was to a different section, and the results were regarded as though the same group had been given three equivalent tests at appropriate intervals. Statistical analyses of several types bore out the validity of this assumption. Yes-no (true-false), four-response and five-response multiple-choice, and completion questions, as well as brief themes, were used in testing motion-picture retention. The five-response multiple-choice question proved to be the type best adapted to the uses of the study. Various factors in the testing techniques employed interfered to produce second- and third-grade test scores which were higher than they should have been in respect to those of older observers. These factors were measurable to a certain extent, but they could not be corrected for with certainty. The methods used in analyzing earlier pictures and in constructing tests for them were retained with certain modifications. By the several methods used the tests were shown to be valid and reliable. The relationship was high between scores on general and specific tests, but low between scores on general or specific tests and chronological age, mental age, or educational age. The questions in the specific tests were classified according to the kind of action occurring at the time and according to the background in which the action occurred. Data from the results of these classifications will be presented in the following chapter.

TABLE V (*Continued*)

AVERAGE PERCENTAGES OF CORRECT RESPONSES, SPECIFIC TESTS

FOR PICTURES 4 TO 16 (*Continued*)

	GRADES 2–3		GRADES 5–6		GRADES 9–10		ADULTS	
	Number	Average (Per Cent)	Number	Average (Per Cent)	Number	Average (Per Cent)	Number	Average (Per Cent)
16. "Stolen Heaven":								
Specific	178	59.5	237	67.0	266	79.2	29	85.5
1½ Specific	52	50.2	84	62.1	143	69.0	...	.....
3 Specific	29	51.0	27	63.8	106	65.6	...	.....
Total Pictures 11 to 16 (1930–31):								
Specific	959	52.2	1,180	65.9	1,270	80.9	162	87.8
1½ Specific	612	47.4	789	58.8	1,017	71.0	122	71.8
3 Specific	426	47.8	524	56.2	838	65.4	109	73.0
Total Pictures 4 to 10 (1929–30):								
Specific	...	52.8	....	42.9	....	53.5	...	64.7
1 Specific	...	56.7	....	38.4	....	42.2	...	51.1
2 Specific	...	51.1	....	....	....	....	...	....

This table may be interpreted as follows: The second-third grade-group answered the Specific test for "Tom Sawyer" 49.4 per cent correctly. A month and a half later an equated group from the same grades and schools answered the same questions 51.2 per cent correctly, a gain of 1.8 per cent of the total percentage or a gain of 3.6 per cent on the original responses. Three months after the picture was seen, a third equated group from the same grades answered the same test 55.0 per cent correctly, a gain of 5.6 per cent of the total or 11.3 per cent of the original responses, and so on.

The specific-information tests have been described in the previous chapters. Glancing through those brief descriptions or analyzing some of the specimen tests included in Appendix I one sees that a main factor in test construction was the preparation of a device for the measurement of reaction to and retention of a picture as a whole. Details were in themselves ignored; test questions which concerned small incidents in a picture were really intended to measure retention of that section of the picture which subtly hinged upon a seemingly minor portion. For example, consider the following item:

> 31. Felice said that when she was married she would be of help to her husband because she had (1) a wagon and horses (2) a lot of linen (3) some money (4) a number of furs (5) some furniture ("Fighting Caravans," Specific No. 31).

Her dowry was more or less immaterial, yet, if the entire situation is understood, this particular dowry becomes of decided importance. Clint, the prospective bridegroom, was a man of the plains, a frontiersman. Freedom meant more to him than any other thing, and the mention of linen had its implications of fixed residence and household duties. He suddenly fled in panic. While on his mad flight away from the caravan, he ran across evidence of the projected Indian attack and returned in time to organize the defense, thereby saving the lives of the members of the caravan. A considerable portion of the plot hinged upon Felice's innocent and apparently unimportant use of the word "linen." Although it might appear unimportant as a test question, in all probability it really tested the recall of a pertinent portion of the picture.

Radossawljewitsch, Ebbinghaus, and others have tested memory span over varying periods of time, and have found retention at the end of a month's time amounting to from 12 to 30 per cent. In this study retention at the end of a month was almost as high as in the original testing immediately after the picture; on occasions the average score of a group was even higher a month or more after than immediately following the picture (see Table V). The technique employed by Ballard is used here. The original retention (the day after the picture) is considered as 100 per cent in each case, and deviations are determined with this as the base.

During the 1930–31 study the time for the later testings was extended to one and one-half and three months, but even with this longer time and with a heterogeneous group of children there are still evidences of high retention. Reference to Table V will show that on "Tom Sawyer" and "Fighting Caravans" an increase occurred in the average scores of this age-group over even the longer interval of one and one-half months. One curious fact is that for "Tom Sawyer" there was still a further increase in the period between the 1½ Specific and 3 Specific tests. The retention of these children on the 1½ Specific was 104 per cent, and on the 3 Specific 111 per cent as high as their scores on the Specific. There was an increase from the 1½ Specific to the 3 Specific also on "Stolen Heaven," and at no point was the drop between these two testings at all large.

A brief analysis of Table VI will show several interesting changes in the percentages of correct responses from testing to testing of the individual items in the six specific tests of 1930–31. The six specific-information tests used in these years contained a total of 240 questions. Out of these a number were remembered better on the 1½ Specific or 3 Specific than on the Specific which followed the picture immediately. This factor of questions which were remembered better at a later day was found more frequently in the tests of second-third grade-groups than in those of the older groups. As an exception, however, it is to be noted that nearly 60 per cent of the time the adults remembered situations better three months after the picture than they did a month and a half after it. When the average scores on the complete tests are considered, these increases are lost sight of unless they occur in sufficient frequency to cause an entire test average on a 1½ Specific or 3 Specific to surpass the average score for the same age-group on the Specific test.

This factor of retention is a major finding of the study and is worthy of further analysis. It was previously thought that children did not understand pictures, in the first place, and did not remember them, in the second. It appears, however, that children do understand pictures. What they see is present in their memories, practically intact, waiting only for a stimulus to arouse it. They will probably never again meet such a stimulus as the tests used in this experiment, but the memories are there. A child goes to a picture for a variety of reasons, but the content of the picture stays with him a long time, without effort on his part. The factors which cause this long-time retention, and even increase, will be discussed in a later paragraph.

As shown in the second section of Table VI, there are frequent questions on which the percentage of correct responses for one age-group is superior to that of an older age-group, although, as shown in Table V, each age-group has a total average percentage of correct responses which is larger than that of each younger group. When the statistical technique involving the probable error of difference is used, these superiorities are found to be in the main statistically significant. Six of the 9 possible comparisons of age-groups to those next younger show differences of 4 or more probable errors of difference and 2 more show differences of

TABLE VI

THE PERCENTAGES OF THE TWO HUNDRED FORTY QUESTIONS IN SIX SPECIFIC TESTS WHICH WERE ANSWERED BETTER ON LATER TESTINGS THAN ON EARLIER ONES, AND WHICH WERE ANSWERED BETTER BY YOUNGER OBSERVERS THAN BY OLDER ONES

	Grades 2-3		Grades 5-6		Grades 9-10		Adult [a]	
	Number of Cases	Per Cent of Items	Number of Cases	Per Cent of Items	Number of Cases	Per Cent of Items	Number of Cases	Per Cent of Items
Answers Better on Later than on Earlier Test								
Higher on the:								
1½ Specific than Specific..	86	35.8	56	23.3	26	10.8	41	20.5
3 Specific than Specific..	87	36.3	42	17.5	11	4.6	26	16.3
3 Specific than 1½ Specific	109	45.4	86	35.8	52	21.7	95	59.4
Answered Better by Younger than Older Observers								
Grades 5-6............	51	21.3 b	..	..	.....	....	...	...
Grades 9-10...........	11	4.6 b	8	3.3	...	....	...	...
Adults................	7	2.9 b	8	3.3	45	18.8	...	...

a Adults did not take one 1½ Specific and two 3 Specific tests; therefore comparisons involving 1½ and 3 Specific tests can be made on but 200 and 160 items, respectively.
b To be interpreted that the second-third grade-group was superior to the group indicated on the number of items and the percentage of the total number (240) as shown.

This table may be interpreted as follows: 35.8 per cent of the time second-third grade-group had higher average percentages of correct responses on the items of the 1½ Specific test than on the same items in Specific tests, and so on. This age-group had higher average scores on items in Specific tests 21.3 per cent of the time than did the fifth-sixth grade-group on these items, and so on.

3.25 *PE* and 3.90 *PE*, which give a high degree of reliability. When total tests are considered, each age-group has higher retention on specific tests than each younger age-group, but it is a different kind of retention. A young child has not the sense of values of an older child or an adult, and he seizes upon some inconsequential detail which has been ignored by the adults. Conversely, young children do not adequately comprehend the plot of a picture and do not grasp or do not remember certain important portions which register automatically with adults and older children. Retention of the material shown on the screen is tremendous for observers of all ages, and unconscious reorganization of data may lead to higher retention over longer periods of time than immediately following the viewing of the picture. This retention is in all probability almost entirely unconscious. It is the type of retention referred to in psychology as "nonvoluntary" learning, which comes without conscious effort on the part of the observer.

A comparison of the retention of children from different localities.—It is difficult in the extreme to evaluate this factor within a short space. In the 1929–30 portion of the study variations between groups of the same age in different localities were not large. There was, however, but little variation in the communities available for the study. In 1930–31 a conscious effort was made to select communities which would yield as wide variations of modes of living and of family incomes as possible. In the list for that year was one of the select residential sections of Cincinnati, an average residential district in Columbus, the poorest district in Cincinnati, the small university town of Delaware, the small town of Wellsburg on the edge of the coal and iron district, and Jackson, a medium-sized city in the agricultural belt of the South. All types of occupations and all types of homes were represented. Taken together, this group forms a well-rounded cross section of American life. Taken separately, the communities provide a wealth of comparative data, worthy of a complete report in themselves.

In comparing the average scores of these six sections of each age-group the probable error of difference is used, and quotients are translated into chances in 100 of an actual superiority as indicated. If the mean score for one group is 45 and for another 53, and the probable error of difference is 2, then the difference between the scores, 8, divided by the probable error of the difference, 2, gives a quotient of 4. This shows a difference of 4 *PE* between the two means, which indicates less than one chance in 100 of the group having the average score of 45 actually being equal to the higher group in respect to the quality being tested.[2]

When the average score of each of the 6 sections of an age-group is compared to every other average score in the age-group, 15 comparisons are available. In order to illustrate the differences existing between the sections of each age-group, these 15 comparisons were made for each of the three age-groups on the average scores of the Specific test for "Passion Flower," making 45 comparisons in all. Sixteen of the 45 are larger than 4 *PE*, showing practical certainty of the superiority of certain sections over certain other sections. There are only 8 differences out of the total 45 which are less than 1 *PE*, a difference which might be expected solely by chance. All the extreme variations (4 *PE* or greater) occur in the second-third and fifth-sixth grade-groups.

[2] Garrett, H. E., *Statistics in Psychology and Education*. New York: Longmans, Green, 1926. Pp. xiii, 317.

Some of the communities showed definite superiorities over others of the group, yet there was no definite trend noticeable in this situation. Children in some of the localities, where living conditions were poor, showed a higher degree of retention than did other communities where conditions were more favorable. The relative standing of the groups of the same age from different localities were frequently reversed on other pictures. As far as this study could determine, none of this superiority of a group from one locality over a group of the same age from another locality could be attributed to the degree of frequency of movie attendance in either locality. Existing differences must have been due then to variations in environment which would cause children in one locality to notice actions and items of conversation or background which would pass unobserved with children of the same age in another locality.

There are two other methods of making this comparison. Each section of an age-group was compared in the same manner to the combined scores of the other sections of the age-groups, making 6 possible comparisons for each age-group, or 18 in all. Six of the 18 showed differences of 4 *PE* or more. These 6 were divided equally between the two youngest age-groups.

In the other method of comparison, the difference between the scores on the Specific test for "Passion Flower" for each pair of adjacent age-groups in each locality was measured in terms of the same yardstick—probable errors. These differences were then compared with the ones described in the earlier paragraphs of this section. For example, the difference between the average scores of the fifth-sixth grade-group and the second-third grade-group of Delaware was compared with the differences between the Delaware fifth-sixth grade and the other fifth-sixth grade-groups. The difference between the average score of each section for each age-group, and the adjacent age-group in the same community was compared to the difference between the section and the other five sections of the same age. As age-groups could be compared to younger ones as well as to older, four sets of comparisons were available, making a total of 120 comparisons. Out of these 120 comparisons, a total of 56, or nearly half, showed greater differences between children of the same grade but of different locality than between children two or more grades apart in the same locality. In other words, the average level of ability to understand and retain the material of this picture which was found in the second-third grade in one locality might not be found in another community until the fifth and sixth grades.

It is a difficult situation to understand. Intelligence, as measured by group tests, did not show a marked difference between localities, and ages were not significantly different. The variations in scores which occurred were frequently in favor of the younger children or children of lower mental or educational ability. The only conclusion which can be drawn is that at any given age or grade-level children from different localities do differ in their reactions to and retention of motion pictures. These variations are not the same for all pictures. Two groups of the same age in different localities may differ on the tests for one picture, and the direction of these differences may be reversed on tests for the next picture. Nor were these chance variations; they were statistically significant. A discussion of the material remembered best, or least, from the pictures may throw more light on this complex situation.

Retention of different kinds of action, types of action, and background.—When the study was initiated, one of the main objectives was an analysis of the factors producing differences in average test scores. If an age-group in a given locality does well on the tests for one picture and not so well on those for another, what factors have caused the change? Why does a group in one locality surpass a group of the same age in another locality in the retention of one picture and not of another? All tests which were used for the pictures were constructed on the basis of the same aims; they were made by the same group and carefully surveyed and revised before use. Several statistical check-ups showed that but few of these variations could be attributed to variations in the tests. These variations occurred as freely when Section A of an age-group was tested on two pictures as when Section A was tested on one and Section B on another. Here were definite variations in the types of things that children remembered, and the actual variations were therefore analyzed to ascertain the causes. If one picture contains a large proportion of romantic incidents which appeal to the children of a certain age in one community but which do not appeal to children of the same age in other communities, it may cause a higher retention of the picture on the part of the former group.

As mentioned in a previous chapter, all questions in the tests of specific information were divided according to the action taking place and also according to the type of action and the background in which the action occurred. These divisions were made carefully by a committee working from a set of written definitions. Ten main kinds of action were shown in the pictures of 1930–31 and from 9 to 51 questions were based on each. Table VII shows the rank of retention of each kind of action, based upon average percentages of retention, for each section at each age-level. There is a considerable variance in the average retention by the sections of each age-group. Sports are remembered best of all kinds of action by the second and third grades of two localities whereas in one locality sports rank next to last in average percentage of retention by this age-group. Definite tendencies are present, however. Sports, general action, and crime are usually remembered by all of the age-groups, while questions involving drinking, bootlegging, and business are not generally well retained.

Many of these data were not, however, statistically significant. When the probable errors of the difference were computed, many of the differences between average percentages of correct responses on two kinds of action when divided by the probable error gave quotients of less than 4 PE. This result was probably due to two factors: First, only 11 classifications were used, a situation which of necessity caused questions of fairly dissimilar type to be included within a single classification. Table VII covers data from 1930–31 only, and, as the classification of items varies slightly from that of the previous years, a combination of the data from the two periods is impossible at this point. Second, there were too few questions in several of the classifications, resulting in a large probable error of the mean for each of these classifications. The formula for the probable error of the mean is

$$PE_M = \frac{.6745\sigma_{\text{dis.}}}{\sqrt{N}}$$

and when N, the number of questions in the category, is only 10 or 12, the probable error is large and the difference between the means of two classifications must needs be large to be statistically significant. If five or ten times as many pictures had been used in the experiment, the

TABLE VII

THE AVERAGE RETENTION OF EACH OF SEVERAL DIFFERENT KINDS OF ACTION BY CHILDREN AT EACH AGE-LEVEL IN EACH COMMUNITY ON TESTS OF SPECIFIC INFORMATION, 1930–31

COMMUNITY	General Action	Crime	Sports	Romantic	Titles	Mystery	General Conversation	Fighting	Social Activities	Business	Drinking
Grades 2–3:											
Jackson (Rank)	2	3	1	6	5	4	10	7	8	9	11
Columbus	3	2	10	7	1	5	6	9	4	11	8
Wellsburg	1	2	6	5	9	8	7	3	10	4	11
Delaware	2	3	1	6	4	5	9	7	10	8	11
Cincinnati (Avondale)	4	1	7	5	6	9	3	2	8	11	10
Cincinnati (Raschig)	1	2	3	4	7	6	8	10	9	5	11
Total (Specific)	1	2	3	4	5	6	7	8	9	10	11
Total (1½ Specific)	2	3	4	5	1	8	9	7	11	6	10
Total (3 Specific)	2	3	4	6	1	8	9	5	11	7	10
Grades 5–6:											
Jackson (Rank)	2	3	1	5	4	7	9	8	5	10	11
Columbus	2	4	1	3	7	8	6	9	5	10	11
Wellsburg	2	3	1	4	8	5	6	7	10	9	11
Delaware	2	3	1	5	6	4	8	10	7	9	11
Cincinnati (Avondale)	4	3	2	4	7	9	6	8	10	5	11
Cincinnati (Raschig)	2	1	1	3	7	9	6	10	5	8	11
Total (Specific)	2	3	1	4	5	6	8	9	7	10	11
Total (1½ Specific)	2	3	1	5	4	6	10	9	7	8	11
Total (3 Specific)	1	3	4	5	2	6	10	8	9	7	11

TABLE IX

AN ANALYSIS OF RETENTION OF ITEMS COVERING THE PLOT
OF THE PICTURE AND INCIDENTAL ITEMS

	MEAN PERCENTAGES OF ITEMS RETAINED			
	Grades 2–3	Grades 5–6	Grades 9–10	Adults
	Five Specific Tests, 1929–30			
Plot:				
Specific	55.1	51.6	61.1	75.9
1 Specific	58.5	48.0	54.1	63.7
Incidental occurrences:				
Specific	49.0	39.0	49.7	58.4
1 Specific	50.7	32.3	37.6	43.2
Retention ratio, plot	106.2	93.0	88.5	83.9
Retention ratio, incidental	103.5	82.8	75.7	74.0
	Six Specific Tests, 1930–31			
1. Plot (essential):				
Specific	53.3	68.6	83.6	90.7
1½ Specific	49.6	62.9	72.4	77.3
3 Specific	48.6	60.4	70.3	79.7
2. Plot (non-essential):				
Specific	49.8	65.0	80.8	86.5
1½ Specific	44.3	54.7	66.8	71.7
3 Specific	42.8	51.6	60.7	74.5
3. Incidental occurrences:				
Specific	48.4	55.2	71.4	80.8
1½ Specific	40.8	41.4	54.4	59.1
3 Specific	39.4	38.7	48.4	60.3
Percentage 1½ Specific is of Specific:				
1. Plot (essential)	93.1	91.7	86.6	85.2
2. Plot (non-essential)	89.0	84.2	82.7	82.9
3. Incidental occurrences	84.3	75.0	76.2	73.1
Percentage 3 Specific is of Specific:				
1. Plot (essential)	91.2	88.0	84.1	87.9
2. Plot (non-essential)	85.9	79.4	75.1	86.1
3. Incidental occurrences	81.4	70.1	67.8	74.6

This table may be read as follows: The second-third grade-group taking
the specific-information tests during 1929–30 retained items concerned with
the plot of the picture 55.1 per cent correctly and incidental items 49.0 per
cent correctly. On the 1 Specific tests this difference is still more pronounced,
and so on.

tions of pictures are remembered better and longer than unimportant ones.[3]

This is neither an astonishing nor an unexpected discovery, but it is one which, in the light of the findings of the previous paragraph, needs to be discussed further. If portions of a picture are deemed important by the makers of the picture, it has been shown that by the process of giving these portions a high emotional tone they can be made to stand out. The important items, the items of a highly emotional type, are remembered better. Is this, however, always to the best interests of the observer? If pictures are constructed ideally and if they contain no incorrectly shown general information, this situation may be acceptable and even laudable. On the other hand, how can we be certain that any given picture is entirely free from propaganda and free from all accidental or premeditated distortion of actual fact? In a later paragraph it will be shown that there is a definite tendency to accept as true general information exhibited incorrectly on the screen. If an emotional scene—a scene of high importance in the plot of the picture—contains misinformation of a general character, this misinformation has great chances of being accepted as true. This statement is particularly true when young children view the picture.

Examples of questions coming in the classification used are:

Plot essential—Tanya came to the fort to (1) make up with Michael (2) laugh at Michael (3) warn Michael (4) get away from Boris (5) whip Michael. ("New Moon," Specific, No. 30.)

(2) Plot non-essential—Joe's head was hurt by (1) broken glass (2) a policeman's club (3) a bullet (4) a rock (5) a sharp knife. ("Stolen Heaven," Specific, No. 3.)

[3] However, it does not follow that unimportant or incidental items are badly remembered. Reference to Table IX shows that there is a high retention for all types of material, especially in the case of the younger children.

tion are attitude questions, a type this study has attempted
to avoid.

Questions for use in a study of this type must be so constructed that only one interpretation of the question can
be made, and so worded that no portion of the question gives
a hint as to the correct answer. Scoring must be so objective that a properly corrected paper will have the same score
each time if given to a number of graders for correction.
Questions must be easy enough for second-grade children
yet difficult enough to be missed occasionally by members
of the group of superior adults. Reliability of information
and objectivity of tests can be controlled with a fair amount
of ease, but the construction of items containing the proper
degree of difficulty was a major problem.

If it is discovered that the misinformation occasionally
shown in motion pictures is frequently accepted as the truth,
an important discovery has been made. In "The Mysterious
Island" there were a number of incidents of a rather fan-
tastic nature which were contrary to the scientific facts of
to-day. A submarine went to the bottom of the ocean at
a depth of two miles; the occupants donned diving suits,
explored, and found a race of undersea people, a huge animal resembling the old dinosaur stegosaurus, and so on.
Half of the questions in the test for older observers were
based upon incorrectly shown action of this type, and the
remaining twenty based upon correctly shown items. Table
XI shows the average percentages of correct responses for
the two types of questions on each administration of the
test, in which 17 items were shown contrary to fact and
13 items shown correctly, each with 20 other items. All
groups show higher percentages of increase on the General
over the Pretest for correctly shown items as compared
to incorrectly shown items. Children in the second-third

grade-group apparently pay less attention to inconsistencies, or understand them less, and are less influenced by them. This analysis shows a distinct influence of motion pictures upon general information.

TABLE XI

A COMPARISON OF PERCENTAGES OF CORRECT RESPONSES ON ITEMS SHOWN CORRECTLY AND ITEMS SHOWN IN-CORRECTLY IN "THE MYSTERIOUS ISLAND," GENERAL–INFORMATION TESTS

TEST	PERCENTAGES OF CORRECT RESPONSE			
	Grades 2–3	Grades 5–6	Grades 9–10	Adult
	Items Shown Contrary to Fact			
Pretest.............................	30.6	29.4	34.1	36.7
General.............................	42.1	36.7	39.8	38.5
1 General.............................	40.0	30.0	36.5	40.4
2 General.............................	42.8	....	....	....
	Items Shown True to Fact			
Pretest.............................	30.8	32.3	49.0	67.7
General.............................	50.2	61.0	66.4	69.7
1 General.............................	54.6	53.3	60.4	73.1
2 General.............................	60.9	....	....	....

This table may be read as follows: The second-third group had approximately equal scores on correctly and incorrectly shown items in the Pretest, but on the General test given the day following the picture, the average percentages of correct responses were considerably higher on the correctly shown items, and so on.

During 1930–31 this factor was taken more carefully into account. Two pictures in particular offered a considerable amount of general information which was far from the truth, as well as it could be determined by careful investigation. In "New Moon" a Russian second lieutenant, a post filled from the peasant class, falls in love with and marries a princess whose uncle (father's brother) is only a count. The second lieutenant is in charge of a company of soldiers and later in charge of an important frontier fortress. Numerous geographical data are wrong as are even some of the physical data, such as the sending of a telegram from the Caspian Sea to Petrograd and the almost instantaneous receipt of the answer. This is a practically impossible accomplishment in present-day America, and is even more so in Russia. In "Fighting Caravans" a tank car of kerosene was hauled by wagon train across the prairies in 1861, whereas kerosene only became something more than a scientific curiosity late in that decade with the advent of the kerosene lamp. It is just as important, if not more so, to determine the reactions of observers to items incorrectly shown as it is to find out how their fund of general information has been increased by correctly shown items. If an item is shown correctly and the percentages of correct responses on that item increase after the picture is seen, there is, at least, partial proof that the picture has had an influence, while if an item is shown incorrectly and the percentages of correct responses decrease appreciably, the corroborating evidence is strong. To make matters doubly sure concerning the reactions to these two types of questions, there was inserted in each of the last three general tests a set of 5 items of exactly the same type as those of the regular test and covering the same subject-matter, but concerned with information not shown in the picture. The observers' reaction to these items was unusual. Presumably, they were puzzled by their inability to answer these items from what they had seen in the picture, and cast around for possible answers from this source. Consequently, there was a higher percentage of these items not answered on the General tests, and the percentages of correct response declined slightly (see Table XII). Items shown incorrectly had considerably lower percentages of correct response on the General tests than on the Pretests.

TABLE XII

AVERAGE PERCENTAGES OF CORRECT RESPONSES—TOTAL OF
ALL GENERAL TESTS, 1930–31

TYPES OF ITEMS	GRADES 2–3	GRADES 5–6	GRADES 9–10	ADULTS
Shown correctly:				
Pretest.................	37.7	36.1	47.8	61.0
General.................	42.2	47.2	64.0	78.2
1½ General.............	42.7	44.1	60.9	71.6
Shown incorrectly:				
Pretest.................	34.9	31.4	41.7	53.0
General.................	32.2	25.4	27.6	33.1
1½ General.............	28.7	25.2	34.2	42.2
Not shown:				
Pretest.................	36.5	30.9	45.6	61.1
General.................	33.3	31.4	38.5	53.6
1½ General.............	34.5	33.6	43.0	55.8
	Percentage of the Pretest			
Shown correctly:				
General.................	111.9	130.7	133.9	128.2
1½ General.............	113.3	122.2	127.4	117.4
Shown incorrectly:				
General.................	92.3	80.9	66.2	62.5
1½ General.............	82.2	80.3	82.0	79.6
Not shown:				
General.................	91.2	101.6	84.4	87.7
1½ General.............	94.5	108.7	94.3	91.3

This table may be read as follows: The second-third grade-group increased
its average scores on items shown correctly 12 per cent between the Pretests
and the General tests. That is, their general information concerning the
topics shown in the pictures increased on the average 12 per cent by seeing
the picture if the items were shown correctly. If the items were shown incorrectly, seeing the picture decreased their general information 8 per cent,
and so on.

One other point should be discussed in connection with
differences in response to correctly and incorrectly shown
items. In the case of "The Mysterious Island" the mean
score on items shown incorrectly rose slightly on the General
as compared to the Pretest, although for none of the school

groups did the rise even approximate that of the mean score of items shown correctly. This rise is easily explained when the character of the picture is taken into account. "The Mysterious Island" is much like a fairy tale; the incongruities in it are so absurd that most people immediately recognize them as fallacious. Therefore, in only a few cases was there an actual decrease in means of incorrectly shown items.

This paragraph joins closely to those covering specific information. The two types of information should really be discussed simultaneously, as the section of a picture from which a specific-information item is taken frequently yields an additional item covering general information. It has been noted that for all ages of observers, but particularly for children of the second and third grades, items of specific information in pictures are sometimes retained better over a longer period of time than over a shorter. This is also true of items of general information. There are cases in which an item of this type has a higher percentage of correct responses on the $1\frac{1}{2}$ General test than on the General test immediately following the picture. Reorganization of the plot of the picture apparently aids retention of the general information contained in the picture.

Summary.—The retention of specific information from motion pictures is high. The retention of second-third grade and older children was 59 per cent or more of that of superior adults. Retention over a period of a month and a half averaged 90 per cent of the amount retained the day after the picture for the three groups of school children and 82 per cent for the adults. On many of the items the retention of a younger group was higher than that of one or more older groups. Sometimes items, or even whole tests, were retained better for a grade-group over a longer period of time than over a shorter. Children in the same grade-groups in different localities varied considerably in their retention of the pictures. A superiority of one locality over another on one picture was frequently reversed in the tests for another picture.

In general, action was remembered best when it concerned items of sports, general action, and crime, when it was somewhat emotional and when it occurred in a familiar type of background, such as home or school. Business, bootlegging, and drinking were not remembered well, nor were items with little emotional appeal nor items occurring in unfamiliar and interesting settings which would attract attention away from the action occurring at the time. Items of major interest to the plot of the story were retained over a short time much better than were incidental items; this superiority increased over a longer period of time. There was little difference in the retention of boys and girls. General information presented by the pictures was retained to a large extent if it was shown correctly in the pictures. These increases ranged from 12 per cent to 34 per cent for the different age-groups. Information shown incorrectly in the pictures was largely accepted. These decreases in general information ranged from 8 per cent to 38 per cent.

CHAPTER IV

A COMPARISON OF THIS STUDY AND
OTHER STUDIES IN LEARNING

A comparison of this study and earlier studies of learning.—
The various phases of memory have long constituted a fruit-
ful field for speculation and theorizing. Some of the scientific
approaches were completed over forty-five years ago—those
of Ebbinghaus during 1879–85—but still have a considerable
amount to contribute to the present-day discussions of the
problem.

Ebbinghaus has carried out the pioneer, and probably
the outstanding, research in memory. Using nonsense sylla-
bles largely, he tested other observers and himself to determine the character of retention over various lengths of
time and under different conditions. His experiments included the introduction of new sets to be learned between
the original learning and the recall, the relearning, the
amount lost being indicated by the time or the number of
repetitions necessary to bring the learning back to its former
degree of excellency. His experiments were carried out under
laboratory conditions, and his material to be memorized
consisted largely of meaningless or uninteresting material.[1]

Since then, Müller, Schumann, Meumann, Radossawljewitsch, and others worked out experiments of a similar nature, improving the techniques of Ebbinghaus. Two methods
of testing the efficiency of the memory are in general use: the
method of correct associates and the saving method. The

[1] Ebbinghaus, H., *Über das Gedachtnis* (translated by Ruger and Bussenius).
New York: Teach. Coll., Columbia Univ., 1913. Pp. 123.

67

former is used to test organization; that is, parts of the learned material are furnished as stimuli and the omitted parts are to be furnished by the observer. In the saving method the amount of practice necessary to relearn the material forgotten during the interim is the measure of the amount retained. This study used the method of correct associates.

Ballard used the students in 42 senior departments of the elementary schools of London in his experiment in the memorization of poetry. He supplied each student with a copy of a 34-line selection which had been read to each class, had it studied briefly, and then asked each pupil to write all he could remember of what he had learned. Ballard divided the 42 departments into 7 equated groups and unexpectedly asked each of the separate groups for repetitions of the writing at periods varying from one to seven days after the original memorization. This procedure was followed in the memorization of several poems, a nonsense verse, diagrams, and the like. In each case, if the amount recalled immediately after the memorization was considered as 100 per cent, the change from this original basis was in the direction of increased retention over periods of one to six days, varying with the type of material learned, the age, sex, intelligence, and experience of the learner. Ballard notes especially the fact that much that was originally learned was forgotten during this period, so that this apparent superiority of the second test over the first really represents an actual superiority plus additional material to make up for that lost. He refers to this new material, the result of the process of maturation, as "reminiscence," which he states may be due to removal of obstructing inhibitions, removal of fatigue due to memorizing, or other causes.[2] Ballard is one of the few

[2] Ballard, P. B., *Obliviscence and Reminiscence*. Brit. J. Psychol. Monog. Suppl. 1913, 1, No. 2. Pp. vii, 82.

who have discovered this maturation effect and noted more than casual interest in it as a portion of a learning experiment. His study is probably closer to this experiment than any of the others reviewed here.

The findings of Ballard's study have been borne out by this one. The authors of this report hesitate to use the word "reminiscence," yet the same condition prevails here as with Ballard. In the case of the retention of earlier pictures by the second-third grade-group and even by older observers, there were found pictures for which the average scores were lower on the Specific or General test administered the day following the picture than were the scores on the same test given to equated groups a month later. This increase was not an increase on all items included in the test. On many items the retention decreased, yet on the rest of the items there was a sufficient increase to more than compensate for the deficiency. Some of this situation shows itself in Table VI.[3]

In all of these experiments there is an emphasis upon the formal technicalities of memorization. The material to be learned is carefully standardized and given to the subject in an exact way. He is usually uninterested in the content, or he carries as a secondary interest in it a wish to please a professor, to pass the course, or to earn the promised sum of money for the time spent. As a usual thing, only the material to be recalled is memorized at the time, although confusion material may be memorized in the interim before recall is requested. Practice is carried forward in most of these experiments until learning is complete, but the mechanical nature of the material memorized causes rather quick forgetting.

In the organization of this problem only one view of the

[3] See page 43.

picture was presented. The pupils saw the entire picture without knowledge of the sections which would be asked in recall, and were present at the show with the attitude of seeking enjoyment rather than of attempting to memorize. Periods of testing were stretched to three months and in one case seven months after the show. Under these conditions results should, and do, differ markedly from those of Ebbinghaus, Meumann, and others.

The percentages of retention over a period of one day as obtained by Radossawljewitsch and by this study are not capable of exact comparison. In the former studies, retention was based upon material which was repeated until learning was just complete, and the percentages given indicate retention of this perfectly learned material. In this study, the children saw each picture once only. Much confusion material, that is, items not covered by test items, was present, including several reels of comedy and news in addition to the feature, and much of this confusion material was indistinguishable from the material to be tested. When these points are understood, it is not peculiar that the one-day testings of the two studies show different results. The real comparison between the two studies lies in the lower section of Table XIII where percentages of long-time retention are based upon one-day retention. The retention found by this study is far higher over a long period of time than is that found by former experimenters.

Experiments with motion pictures.—Psychological experiments using motion pictures have been few. There have been a number of studies in the usefulness of movies for the purpose of visual instruction, which will not be reviewed here as they are fairly numerous, similar in type, and far from the present study in method and aim. Jones has completed probably the only study which merits description.

He worked with eight villages in Vermont, using the ordinary audiences which were attracted by free movies. Immediately after the show he turned on the lights and tested retention by the use of multiple-choice and completion questions. His results showed that the curve of retention increased from the age of ten, the lowest age included in the study, to adulthood and declined somewhat after the age of forty.[4] In another section of the study he attempted to determine the efficiency of motion-picture tests as measures of intelligence, finding correlation coefficients with Army Alpha of .621 to .712 with small probable errors.[5]

Mitchell made an analysis of the movie attendance of 10,052 Chicago children of three types, delinquents in detention homes, normal children, and Boy and Girl Scouts. She attempted to analyze the motives which led to movie attendance and drew inferences from the records of movie attendance and types and ages of children. Throughout her book, she emphasizes the strong relationship of delinquency and frequent attendance at motion pictures. She says:

> The extent to which a child is exposed to the movies is in direct proportion to certain factors that enter his life. Delinquent children attend the movies more frequently than do other children. Scouts go to the movies less frequently than do other children, but they go regularly. The only difference between the movie attendance of a child who has directed interests in his life and the child whose recreation is left to his own guidance is in degree.[6]

[4] Jones, Harold Ellis, Conrad, Herbert, and Horn, Aaron, *Psychological Studies of Motion Pictures. II: Observation and Recall as a Function of Age.* University of California Publications in Psychology, 1918–1929 (1928 No. 6), 3, 225–243.

[5] Conrad, Herbert S., and Jones, Harold Ellis, *Psychological Studies of Motion Pictures. III: Fidelity of Report as a Measure of Adult Intelligence.* University of California Publications in Psychology, 1918–1929 (1929 No. 7), 3, 245–276.

[6] Mitchell, Alice Miller, *Children and Movies.* Chicago: Univ. Chicago Press, 1929. Pp. xxiv, 181. (P. 28.)

TABLE XIII

A COMPARISON OF THE RETENTION OF MEANINGFUL MATE-
RIAL FOUND IN THE EXPERIMENTS OF RADOSSAWLJE-
WITSCH AND OF THAT FOUND IN THESE
EXPERIMENTS

EXPERIMENT	SPE-CIFIC	1 SPE-CIFIC	1½ SPE-CIFIC	3 SPE-CIFIC	7 SPE-CIFIC
	Percentages of Retention				
Radossawljewitsch:					
Children	79.0	24.3	....	....	....
Adults	79.7	23.9	....	....	....
Six Specific Tests:					
Grades 2–3	52.2	....	47.4	47.8	....
Grades 5–6	65.9	....	58.8	56.2	....
Grades 9–10	80.9	....	71.0	65.4	....
Adult	87.8	....	71.8	73.0	....
"Why Bring That Up?" [a]					
Grades 2–3	49.4	50.4	....	....	46.8
Grades 5–6	47.5	37.1	....	....	33.9
Grades 9–10	56.5	45.1	....	....	32.2
Adult	66.8	49.3	....	....	45.0
	Percentages of Retention, Considering the Amount Retained One Day as 100 Per Cent				
Radossawljewitsch:					
Children	....	30.8	....	....	....
Adults	....	30.0	....	....	....
Six Specific Tests:					
Grades 2–3	....	....	90.8	91.6	....
Grades 5–6	....	....	89.2	85.3	....
Grades 9–10	....	....	87.8	80.8	....
Adult	....	....	81.8	83.1	....
"Why Bring That Up?"					
Grades 2–3	....	102.0	....	....	94.7
Grades 5–6	....	78.1	....	....	71.4
Grades 9–10	....	79.9	....	....	57.0
Adult	....	74.0	....	....	67.4

[a] Tests for this picture were repeated seven months after the picture, with the results given in this table.

This table may be interpreted as follows: In the experiments of Radossawl-jewitsch, retention over a month's time amounted to but 30 per cent of the amount retained the day following the original learning. In this experiment, retention of a similar character amounted to from 82 per cent to 91 per cent over the period of a month and a half, and so on.

The majority of children come in contact with the movies once or twice a week. Any institution that touches the life of a child with this persistent regularity becomes of high importance to his welfare. Delinquent children attend movies more often than other children, go more frequently at night, and attend without their parents a larger percentage of the time. However, in her concluding paragraph she states,

> The delinquent child's extensive contact with the movie may or may not be due to the fact that he is a delinquent and because of the things back of his delinquency. Whether or not the movie enters into his delinquency is a subject for further research and is out of the realm of this study. The present data only show that the delinquent does have a wider movie experience than do the other children studied.[7]

The present investigation is part of the first real attempt at the evaluation of the effect of motion pictures. Porter working in conjunction with the authors arrived at several interesting conclusions with regard to the memory of primary-school children upon attending movies. These were discussed in conjunction with the results of this study.[8]

The possible utilization of these findings by several fields related to educational psychology.—These findings will naturally be of more interest to educational psychologists than to the students of any other field of knowledge, as the experiment is concerned primarily with phases of the learning problem. There are, however, various related fields which borrow generously from educational psychology, and the contribution of this study to each of these fields is given here briefly.

1. Education.—The use of slides, stereopticans, and motion pictures in visual education has been increasing rapidly

[7] *Op. cit.*, p. 142.
[8] Porter, Elfa McWilliam, *The Curve of Retention in Moving Pictures for Young Children.* State University of Iowa, Unpublished Master's Thesis, 1930. Pp. 119.

in the past decade. This study was not concerned with educational pictures, yet the fact that tremendous retention of scenes and action from ordinary motion pictures was found may lead to an increased use of motion pictures as teaching devices. The retention found here would probably not be duplicated in strictly educational pictures, yet the added incentive present in the classroom, the possibility of reshowing of pictures, and the careful description of each action as it occurs in the educational picture might compensate for the difference between the educational film and the one used for entertainment only. Many pictures marketed for their entertainment value possess tremendous possibilities from a purely educational standpoint. Such pictures as "Simba," "Rango," "Chang," "Nanook of the North," "With Byrd at the South Pole," "The Four Feathers," and others have better teaching possibilities than hours of study on geography lessons. Such pictures as "Abraham Lincoln," "Scaramouche," "The Birth of a Nation," and "The Ten Commandments" present historical facts in a clear and easily understood manner although incorrect action is frequently introduced.

Many of our present-day trends in speech, clothing, and house furnishings are directly attributable to motion pictures. Pictures contribute a considerable amount to our scientific information, but much of this contribution is fallacious and, therefore, worse than useless. Some of the pictures produced for entertainment purposes could legitimately be transported into the schoolroom and used as teaching devices.

2. Child welfare.—Various organized groups of interested persons make monthly reports of pictures recommended for children. Certain pictures are not recommended because of items deemed by the reviewer to be undesirable and harm-

ful. The findings of this study as to the kinds and types of action best and least remembered and the amounts of retention of both specific and general information might well assist in placing these reviews on a reliable basis. Those who review motion pictures for censorship boards or for various social-service agencies might be interested in the findings of this study for the same reason.

The possible effect of these findings on motion pictures.— If these findings are utilized by the motion-picture industry, two results will occur: First, the pictures will be more carefully scrutinized for incongruities and misinformation. One of the chief duties of assistant directors is to make certain of the authenticity of all portions of pictures, yet this duty is frequently slighted. Various items of misinformation are occasionally necessary, but as far as possible these should be so shown that their lack of validity is quite apparent. Second, many pictures prepared for regular theater showings might well be exhibited as regular classroom work. A closer coöperation between producers and educators would be necessary to bring about this innovation.

Summary.—The findings of the study have possible value in their contribution to the general field of learning and retention, as the percentages here obtained were considerably higher than those obtained by previous investigators in the field of retention. Motion pictures appear to have more of a possible contribution to visual education than was previously suspected. Many pictures made for their power to attract box-office receipts have real value in the fields of English, history, and geography. The findings of this study may be of benefit to various boards of motion-picture review. There is at present a real opportunity for producers to show selected pictures in school for the sake of their educational value as well as their entertainment.

CHAPTER V

SUMMARY AND CONCLUSIONS

A brief review of testing techniques.—This study has been carried out with two principal aims in view: to measure the amount and types of information concerning the specific action and background of selected motion pictures which are retained over periods ranging from one day to three months, and to measure the amount and types of general information received from selected motion pictures which are retained over periods ranging from one day to a month and a half. Seventeen pictures were used in the study. For each of these, with one exception, a specific-information test was constructed and given to a third of the observers a day after the exhibition of the picture, was repeated for another third a month or a month and a half later, and for the remaining third was repeated two or three months later. The three groups of observers were equated on the basis of age, mental age, educational age, and all other available measurements. Observers were obtained from the second and third grades, the fifth and sixth grades, the ninth and tenth grades, and superior adults. The second-third grade-group was tested with abbreviated forms of the tests used for older observers.

The same groups were used for tests of general information. Each test was given as a Pretest before the picture to one group; it was given to another group the day following the picture; and it was repeated with the third group a month or a month and a half later. For tests of both types of information the groups were rotated, Group A taking the specific-information test for one picture the day after the exhibition, for the next picture a month and a half after the exhibition, and for the next picture three months after the exhibition.

Nearly 3,000 observers have assisted for one or more tests. There were in all 26 tests consisting of from 30 to 64 items each administered in the aggregate for more than 20,000 testings. A total of over 813,000 items was attempted.

Conclusions drawn from the data of preceding chapters.— Several assumptions concerning equating of groups, combination of data from tests of several pictures, and other techniques were made at the beginning of the study, but all were proved empirically during the progress of the study. The tests used were entirely objective; they made satisfactory provision for an extreme range of talent and were reliable and valid. All statistical procedures necessary to determine these facts and also the conclusions of the following paragraphs have been computed. The following conclusions may therefore be drawn from the data which have been presented:

1. The general information of children and adults is increased to a considerable extent by correctly shown information from motion pictures. On the tests of general information used in this study, the average scores of the groups from the second and third grades, the fifth and sixth grades, the ninth and tenth grades, and the superior adults increased 11.9 per cent, 30.7 per cent, 33.9 per cent, and 28.2 per cent, respectively. This retention is lasting, the percentages of increase between the Pretest and the same test given a month and a half after the exhibition being nearly as large as those obtained the day after the picture.

2. General information presented incorrectly by the pictures is frequently accepted as valid unless the incongruity is quite apparent. For the four age-groups, decreases in average scores on the general-information tests amounted to 7.7 per cent, 19.1 per cent, 33.8 per cent, and 37.5 per cent, respectively, when information was shown incorrectly. These decreases were relatively lasting, even increasing for the two youngest age-groups and decreasing somewhat for the two older age-groups. The content of a picture is accepted as authentic by a large percentage of the audience unless the errors contained are glaring.

3. Retention of the specific incidents of motion pictures is high. Children, even very young ones, can retain specific memories of a picture with a high degree of accuracy and completeness. The second-third grade-group retained on the average nearly 60 per cent as much as the group of superior adults. This retention of scenes from motion pictures is high over a long period of time. A third of each age-group was not tested for three months after each picture, yet the average scores for these groups were 91.6 per cent, 85.3 per cent, 80.8 per cent, and 83.1 per cent as high, respectively, for the second and third grades, the fifth and sixth grades, the ninth and tenth grades, and the adults as they were for equated groups at each age-level the day after the picture. On many individual items the average percentage of correct responses of a younger age-group was higher than that of one or more older age-groups.

4. On some individual test items and occasionally on entire tests, an age-group had a higher average retention on tests a month and a half or three months after the picture than it did the day after the picture. This situation occurred most frequently in the second and third grades, but it was common with all three of the older groups. Although a

picture may seem to fade from consciousness quite rapidly, when the proper stimulus (the test) is used the retention is remarkably high, and because of a settling out of unimportant details it may be remembered even better than at first.

5. Action was remembered best when it concerned activities such as sports, general action, crime, and fighting; when it had a high emotional appeal; and when it occurred in a familiar type of surrounding, such as home, school, or tenement. Action was understood least when it concerned unfamiliar activities such as bootlegging and business; when it had practically no emotional elements; and when it occurred in surroundings of an unfamiliar and interesting type, such as café and frontier.

6. Portions of the picture which were concerned directly with the plot of the story were remembered better by all age-groups the day after the picture than were items concerned with incidental details such as clothes, background, and casual speeches. This superiority increased over the period of a month and a half, and it increased still further on the tests three months after the exhibitions. The important items were remembered better initially; this superiority increased with the passage of time.

7. There was little or no difference in the retention of boys and girls in this study.

8. These high retentions occur with children in a detention home as well as with normal children.

9. The percentages of retention found by this study surpass to a large degree the percentages previously obtained from learning experiments. This is true in spite of the fact that in this experiment the incentive to learn was absent; the material to be learned was not even identified amid the mass of confusion items; and there was but one exhibition

of each picture which occurred in a noisy theater filled with friends of the observers. Each of these points is in direct contrast to the elaborate procedures in use in other experiments in learning.

10. Certain of these findings may prove to be of value to the fields of education and child welfare, and to the motion-picture industry itself.

APPENDIX I

SAMPLES OF TESTS

"NEW MOON"

A Specific Test

The following sentences describe some of the action or setting of the movie. In each sentence select the answer which you think is correct or which comes closest to being the correct one. Notice its number and put a cross in the circle which has the same number as the correct answer. Here is a sample, not taken from the movie.

The capital of Ohio is (1) Dayton (2) Cincinnati (3) Cleveland (4) Columbus (5) Toledo.

1( )   2( )   3( )   4(×)   5( )

In this case, Columbus, number 4, is the correct answer, so there is a cross in circle 4. *Mark only one answer for each question.*

Do not hurry. These answers do not affect your school grades; we just want to find out what you liked about the movie as shown by what you remember about it.

If you forget who was who in the picture, look at this list.

Michael—the lieutenant
Tanya—the princess
Boris—the governor
Igor—the count
Potkin—the orderly

1. The actor who played the lead in this picture was (1) John Boles (2) Ramon Navarro (3) Ronald Colman (4) Dennis King (5) Lawrence Tibbett.   1( )   2( )   3( )   4( )   5( )

2. Potkin gave the peasant girl (1) a cigarette (2) a cookie (3) a parrot (4) a bracelet (5) an apple.

1( )   2( )   3( )   4( )   5( )

3. When the princess watched the people on the lower deck, Michael said he thought she might be angry because (1) he had his coat off (2) he had his arm around a peasant girl (3) he was amusing the

81

peasants   (4) he had not noticed her before   (5) he was eating an apple.   1( )   2( )   3( )   4( )   5( )

4. Potkin, the orderly for Michael, was hurt several times when   (1) he fell out of his bunk   (2) he hit the back of his head on a window   (3) he slipped and fell down   (4) his chair tipped over backwards   (5) Michael knocked him down.

1( )   2( )   3( )   4( )   5( )

5. When the princess asked Michael to sing the gypsy song in English, he   (1) sang it with the right English words   (2) sang it with some other English words   (3) refused to sing it   (4) sang it in gypsy words   (5) played it on the piano.

1( )   2( )   3( )   4( )   5( )

6. When the princess asked Michael to translate the song for her, he said,   (1) "It is a 'naughty' song"   (2) "I don't know what it means"   (3) "Some of the words are not in our language"   (4) "I have forgotten it"   (5) "I have to leave now."

1( )   2( )   3( )   4( )   5( )

7. When Michael said he had almost forgotten she was a princess, Tanya replied,   (1) "What can I do to help you forget?"   (2) "You should never forget"   (3) "I am not a princess to you"   (4) "I cannot forget"   (5) "A soldier should know better."

1( )   2( )   3( )   4( )   5( )

8. When the uncle saw Michael in the princess' room, he   (1) told him to leave before anyone saw him   (2) told his wife that everything was all right   (3) sent for the captain   (4) told his wife to go to the princess' room   (5) told Tanya to send Michael away.

1( )   2( )   3( )   4( )   5( )

9. On the deck the last night on board, Tanya said that it was fun   (1) fooling the people on board   (2) singing for the people   (3) pretending she did not love Michael   (4) throwing away Michael's cigarettes   (5) getting to Krasnov.

1( )   2( )   3( )   4( )   5( )

10. When the people on the boat asked the princess to sing, she and Michael sang   (1) "I Love You Truly"   (2) "Venetian Love Song"   (3) "One Alone"   (4) "Wanting You"   (5) "Volga Boat Song."

1( )   2( )   3( )   4( )   5( )

11. The princess refused to sing more than one song because   (1) she did not like the people who asked her   (2) she wanted to be with Michael   (3) she was tired and wanted to sleep   (4) her aunt told her to leave   (5) she did not want to stay with Michael.

1( )   2( )   3( )   4( )   5( )

12. The countess said that the count had married her because (1) he loved her (2) she had a lot of money (3) she was beautiful (4) her father was a nobleman (5) he thought she was rich.

1( ) 2( ) 3( ) 4( ) 5( )

13. The countess knew that her husband was hiding something from her since (1) he drank so much (2) he laughed too much (3) he called her "baby" (4) he could not keep his mind on the cards (5) he wanted to go for a walk on deck.

1( ) 2( ) 3( ) 4( ) 5( )

14. Boris gave the soldiers forty-eight hours leave in honor of (1) his recent election as governor (2) their successful voyage (3) his engagement to Tanya (4) their bravery in fighting (5) the Emperor's birthday.

1( ) 2( ) 3( ) 4( ) 5( )

15. One of the songs which is sung in this picture is (1) "Russian Lullaby" (2) "Love Is Only a Dream" (3) "Woman Is Fickle" (4) "Lover Come Back to Me" (5) "Cossack Love Song."

1( ) 2( ) 3( ) 4( ) 5( )

16. Potkin said that as far as women were concerned, a man should (1) give them everything they asked for (2) let them entirely alone (3) get all the kissing and cooking he could (4) watch out for them all the time (5) take them or leave them, just as he pleased.

1( ) 2( ) 3( ) 4( ) 5( )

17. Potkin said that when any man talked about women, it reminded him of (1) the lion and the mouse (2) the king who married a peasant girl (3) the song about the farmer's daughter (4) the peasant who was angry with a city (5) the fox who could not reach the grapes.

1( ) 2( ) 3( ) 4( ) 5( )

18. Potkin said that his wife had fallen in love with him because (1) he had money (2) he was a soldier (3) he had saved her life (4) he brought her apples (5) he knocked her down.

1( ) 2( ) 3( ) 4( ) 5( )

19. Potkin said that a man who went to the Governor's ball without an invitation would be (1) shot at sunrise (2) hanged by the thumbs (3) sent to Siberia (4) court-martialed (5) put on guard duty for a long time.

1( ) 2( ) 3( ) 4( ) 5( )

20. The count told Tanya that if she married for money, she should (1) be sure she loved the man (2) let Michael alone (3) be sure she got the money (4) forget all about love (5) get it and then do what she pleased.

1( ) 2( ) 3( ) 4( ) 5( )

21. When Tanya and Boris were in the music room, she started to leave but decided to stay if he would (1) promote Michael (2) announce their wedding soon (3) open the window (4) make love to her (5) leave the door open.

            1( )   2( )   3( )   4( )   5( )

22. When Boris and Tanya were in the music room together, he said that he hoped (1) Tanya would always love him (2) he could bear to wait for the wedding (3) Michael would not cause any trouble (4) he was the man Tanya had been singing of (5) Tanya could dance as well as she sang.

            1( )   2( )   3( )   4( )   5( )

23. When Michael danced with Tanya at the ball, she asked if he had come there to (1) carry her off (2) fight Boris (3) announce their engagement (4) sing (5) make a scene.

            1( )   2( )   3( )   4( )   5( )

24. Tanya tried to protect Michael by saying he came to (1) protect the guests against bandits (2) wish them happiness (3) bring a message (4) return her bracelet (5) say goodbye.

            1( )   2( )   3( )   4( )   5( )

25. The reward Boris offered Michael for his service to the princess was (1) a kiss from the princess (2) money (3) promotion in the army (4) a medal (5) an invitation to the wedding.

            1( )   2( )   3( )   4( )   5( )

26. Michael insulted Tanya by (1) singing a song (2) getting drunk (3) dancing with her (4) coming through the window (5) kissing her.   1( )   2( )   3( )   4( )   5( )

27. When Michael went to the dance, he sang a song which said (1) "Kill your sweetheart" (2) "I want you to love me" (3) "Now is the time for love" (4) "Men are made for war" (5) "If your sweetheart leaves you, be brave."

            1( )   2( )   3( )   4( )   5( )

28. Michael knew there was something wrong at Fort Darvaz because (1) he met some soldiers and loose horses (2) a message was sent to him (3) no flag was flying and the gate was open (4) there were bodies in the road (5) he heard shots and yells.

            1( )   2( )   3( )   4( )   5( )

29. Michael told the native soldiers that they lacked the final mark of bravery which was the ability to (1) laugh at death (2) obey orders (3) attack at night (4) fight with swords (5) drill regularly.   1( )   2( )   3( )   4( )   5( )

30. Tanya came to the Fort to (1) make up with Michael (2) laugh at Michael (3) warn Michael (4) get away from Boris (5) whip Michael.   1( )   2( )   3( )   4( )   5( )

31. Michael said that the Turkomans fought at close range with (1) knives (2) pistols (3) clubs (4) spears (5) revolvers.
                                  1( )   2( )   3( )   4( )   5( )

32. When Tanya found out the danger they were in at the Fort, she (1) tried to make the soldiers fight (2) wanted to leave (3) wished Boris would come (4) was glad she hurt Michael (5) told Michael she was sorry.   1( )   2( )   3( )   4( )   5( )

33. Before Michael went out to fight, he gave Tanya a (1) map (2) rope (3) ring (4) gun (5) knife.
                                  1( )   2( )   3( )   4( )   5( )

34. The soldiers refused to help Michael attack the Turkomans because (1) they were afraid (2) they thought they had a better chance inside the Fort (3) they were afraid to follow Michael (4) they thought the Governor was coming with help (5) they did not want to leave the Fort unguarded.
                                  1( )   2( )   3( )   4( )   5( )

35. When the soldiers refused to follow Michael in an attack he (1) sang a song to them (2) shot two of them (3) gave them money (4) went without them (5) made fun of them.
                                  1( )   2( )   3( )   4( )   5( )

36. The Russian soldiers attacked the Turkomans by (1) creeping up from rock to rock (2) shooting at them from long range (3) rolling rocks down on them (4) attacking on horseback (5) making a bayonet charge.   1( )   2( )   3( )   4( )   5( )

37. When Boris saw Tanya and Michael riding and singing together, he (1) left the Fort (2) wept (3) took Tanya to her room (4) drank a toast to them (5) ordered his soldiers to seize Michael.
                                  1( )   2( )   3( )   4( )   5( )

38. When Tanya heard Michael and the troops returning to the Fort, she (1) ran to meet him (2) returned to town (3) called Boris (4) hid (5) escaped in the opposite direction.
                                  1( )   2( )   3( )   4( )   5( )

39. The count said that a military man's way of starting the day off was to (1) eat a steak for breakfast (2) kill his own breakfast (3) fire a machine gun (4) look around for enemies (5) kiss a girl.
                                  1( )   2( )   3( )   4( )   5( )

40. When Tanya decided that Michael had been killed, she (1) sang a song to the soldiers (2) went to her room and cried (3) asked Boris to take her away (4) started to go and look for him (5) asked her uncle to look for him.

1( )   2( )   3( )   4( )   5( )

41. What actor did you like the best? (1) Igor (2) Tanya (3) Boris (4) Potkin (5) Michael.

1( )   2( )   3( )   4( )   5( )

42. At what time did you like Michael most? When he (1) sang to his soldiers on the boat (2) sang with the princess (3) came to the ball (4) took command of the Fort (5) led his men to the attack.

1( )   2( )   3( )   4( )   5( )

A GENERAL TEST

The questions given below are very general in type. Please answer each one the best you can, and give whatever answer you think is correct, regardless of where you learned the answer. In each sentence select the answer which you think is correct or which comes closest to being the correct one. Notice its number, and put a cross in the circle which has the same number as the correct answer. Here is a general sample.

The capital of Ohio is (1) Dayton (2) Cincinnati (3) Cleveland (4) Columbus (5) Toledo.

1( )   2( )   3( )   4(X)   5( )

In this case, Columbus, number 4, is the correct answer, so there is a cross in circle 4. *Mark only one answer for each question.*

Do not hurry. These answers do not affect your school grades; we want to find out what sort of things you are interested in as shown by what you remember about them.

Most of the following questions apply to Russia before the World War. For all these questions remember what Russian conditions were like and answer the best you can, regardless of where you learned the information.

1. A Russian army officer would be most likely to be punished for (1) kissing a girl in public (2) failing to return the salute of a private (3) being out of uniform (4) eating where his soldiers could see him (5) drinking while on duty.

1( )   2( )   3( )   4( )   5( )

2. A Russian governor who gave a dance would ask (1) the important government officials (2) all important men in the district (3) all important officials, business men, army officers and nobility (4) all the soldiers and officials (5) all the people in the district.

1( )   2( )   3( )   4( )   5( )

3. A cheap, coarse song is called (1) vulgar (2) jazz (3) popular
(4) comic (5) risqué. 1( )   2( )   3( )   4( )   5( )

4. In Russia the poor people had a drink called (1) sake (2) bene-
dictine (3) absinthe (4) ale (5) vodka.
1( )   2( )   3( )   4( )   5( )

5. The Khirgiz and Cossack tribesmen of southeastern Russia wear
(1) turbans (2) round caps (3) tall hats made of sheep skin (4)
tall crowned straw hats (5) handkerchiefs over their heads.
1( )   2( )   3( )   4( )   5( )

6. If a man wanted to be a high officer in the Russian army, he not only
had to be capable, but also be (1) a nobleman (2) rich (3) the
son of a soldier (4) the son of a tradesman (5) a peasant.
1( )   2( )   3( )   4( )   5( )

7. The ruler of Russia in 1913 was called (1) king (2) president
(3) kaiser (4) dictator (5) tsar.
1( )   2( )   3( )   4( )   5( )

8. A brave Russian soldier might be decorated with the (1) Victoria
Cross (2) Croix de Guerre (3) Order of Malta (4) Cross of St.
Vladimir (5) Iron Cross.
1( )   2( )   3( )   4( )   5( )

9. Russian peasant women usually wore on their heads (1) lace caps
(2) kerchiefs (3) straw bonnets (4) winged linen caps (5) felt
hats.   1( )   2( )   3( )   4( )   5( )

10. Russian writing looks a good deal like that of (1) German (2)
English (3) Swedish (4) French (5) Greek.
1( )   2( )   3( )   4( )   5( )

11. Russian soldiers wear uniforms much like (1) German soldiers (2)
French colonials (3) American sailors (4) Scotch soldiers (5)
Riff soldiers.   1( )   2( )   3( )   4( )   5( )

12. One body of water in Russia is the (1) Bay of Bengal (2) Caspian
Sea (3) Lake Chad (4) Dead Sea (5) Bay of Biscay.
1( )   2( )   3( )   4( )   5( )

13. The religion of most of the people of Russia is (1) Roman Catholic
(2) Moslem (3) Protestant (4) Greek Catholic (5) Buddhist.
1( )   2( )   3( )   4( )   5( )

14. In Russia, one of the mountain ranges is the (1) Apennines (2)
Kenya (3) Chiricahua (4) Andes (5) Caucasus.
1( )   2( )   3( )   4( )   5( )

15. When a Russian army officer attended a formal dance, he usually wore (1) a Tuxedo (2) a full dress suit (3) his usual uniform (4) a dress uniform (5) business suit.
1( ) 2( ) 3( ) 4( ) 5( )

16. A commissioned Russian army officer showed his rank and the number of his regiment on an ornament on his (1) shoulder (2) arm (3) neck (4) breast (5) cap.
1( ) 2( ) 3( ) 4( ) 5( )

17. A man who tried to conquer Russia and failed was (1) Charlemagne (2) Napoleon (3) Achilles (4) Wellington (5) Mussolini.
1( ) 2( ) 3( ) 4( ) 5( )

18. On a Russian boat, the steerage (poorer) passengers usually amuse themselves by (1) playing bridge (2) listening to a concert (3) listening to a radio (4) dancing and singing (5) playing games such as deck tennis. 1( ) 2( ) 3( ) 4( ) 5( )

19. Enemies who attack the Russians a great deal are the (1) Turkomans (2) Italians (3) Albanians (4) Montenegrans (5) Swedes.
1( ) 2( ) 3( ) 4( ) 5( )

20. A general who did not like one of his officers could get rid of him easily by (1) putting him in prison (2) shooting him (3) sending him into exile (4) giving him some very dangerous work (5) making him get married. 1( ) 2( ) 3( ) 4( ) 5( )

21. A Russian priest would usually perform a marriage in (1) Latin (2) Russian (3) English (4) part English and part Latin (5) Russian and Latin. 1( ) 2( ) 3( ) 4( ) 5( )

22. The number of witnesses at a wedding under the Greek Catholic faith must be at least (1) one (2) two (3) three (4) four (5) five. 1( ) 2( ) 3( ) 4( ) 5( )

23. After a man had given a message to be sent by telegraph, the time it would take to send it is (1) half minute (2) about one minute (3) several minutes (4) half hour (5) an hour.
1( ) 2( ) 3( ) 4( ) 5( )

24. One language which practically no high-class Russians spoke was (1) French (2) German (3) English (4) Gypsy (5) Slavic.
1( ) 2( ) 3( ) 4( ) 5( )

25. A city in southeastern Russia is (1) Krasnov (2) Riga (3) Tiflis (4) Budapest (5) Oslo. 1( ) 2( ) 3( ) 4( ) 5( )

39. When Mary and Joe met Steve on the beach, she gave him (1) a kiss (2) a handkerchief (3) the envelope of money (4) her coat (5) a ring. 1( ) 2( ) 3( ) 4( ) 5( )

40. The reason Steve told the policeman he would help Joe get free from the charge was (1) Steve was in love with Mary (2) Steve thought Joe was innocent (3) Mary had paid money for his help (4) Steve owed Joe some money (5) Steve expected Mary to go with him. 1( ) 2( ) 3( ) 4( ) 5( )

41. At the close of the picture, we saw Joe arrested for stealing the money. He was probably (1) set free (2) freed on probation (3) put in jail for a couple of years (4) put in jail for ten or fifteen years (5) hanged. 1( ) 2( ) 3( ) 4( ) 5( )

42. At what point in the picture did you like Mary the best? When she (1) took in a man off the street (2) hid a man from the police (3) gambled away the last thousand dollars (4) accepted the money from Steve (5) told Joe they would go to jail to pay for the crime. 1( ) 2( ) 3( ) 4( ) 5( )

43. In what part of the picture did you like Joe the best? When he (1) was able to rob the factory (2) got away from the police (3) started to shoot himself (4) asked another man to take care of Mary (5) decided to give back the money. 1( ) 2( ) 3( ) 4( ) 5( )

APPENDIX II

BIBLIOGRAPHY

1. BALCOLM, A. G.: "The Film as a Medium of Instruction," *Journal of National Education Association*, 1924, 13, 331–332.
2. BALLARD, PHILIP BOSWOOD: "Obliviscence and Reminiscence," *British Journal of Psychology Monograph Supplements*, 1913, 1, No. 2, pp. vii, 82.
3. BASSETT, SARAH JANET: "Retention of History in the Sixth, Seventh and Eighth Grades with Special Reference to the Factors that Influence Retention," *Johns Hopkins University Studies in Education*, 1928, No. 12, pp. viii, 110.
4. BEAN, C. H.: "The Curve of Forgetting," *Archives of Psychology*, 1912, 3, No. 21, pp. iii, 45.
5. BROWN, WARNER: "Effects of Interval on Recall," *Journal of Experimental Psychology*, 1924, 7, 469–474.
6. CHARCOT, JEAN MARTIN: *Leçons sur les Maladies due Système Nerveux*, 3 vols. Paris: Bureau du Progrès Médical, 1890–1894.
7. CONRAD, HERBERT S., and JONES, HAROLD ELLIS: *Psychological Studies of Motion Pictures. III: Fidelity of Report as a Measure of Adult Intelligence*, University of California Publications in Psychology, 1918–1929 (1929, No. 7), 3, 245–276.
8. DALLENBACH, KARL M.: "The Measurement of Attention," *American Journal of Psychology*, 1913, 24, 465–507.
9. EBBINGHAUS, HERMANN: *Memory: A Contribution to Experimental Psychology*, translated by Henry A. Ruger and Clara E. Bussenius. New York: Teachers College, Columbia University, 1913, pp. iii, viii, 123.
10. *Educational Screen*, files from 1924 (Vol. 3) to date.
11. FINKENBINDER, E. O.: "The Curve of Forgetting," *American Journal of Psychology*, 1913, 24, 8–32.
12. GARRETT, HENRY E.: *Statistics in Psychology and Education*. New York: Longmans, Green, 1926, pp. xiii, 317.
13. HENDERSON, E. N.: "A Study of Memory for Connected Trains of Thought," *Psychological Review Monograph Supplement*, 1903, 5, No. 6, pp. iv, 94.
14. JONES, HAROLD ELLIS; CONRAD, HERBERT; and HORN, AARON: *Psychological Studies of Motion Pictures. II: Observation and Re-*

call as a Function of Age, University of California Publications in Psychology, 1918–1929 (1928, No. 6), 3, 225–243.

15. KUHLMANN, F.: "On the Analysis of the Memory Consciousness for Pictures of Familiar Objects," *American Journal of Psychology*, 1907, 18, 389–420.

16. LACY, JOHN V.: "The Relative Value of Motion Pictures as an Educational Agency: An Experimental Study," *Teachers College Record*, 1919, 20, 452–465.

17. LEE, ANG LANFEN: "An Experimental Study of Retention and Its Relation to Intelligence," *Psychological Monographs*, 1925, 34, No. 4, pp. x, 45.

18. LUH, C. W.: "The Conditions of Retention," *Psychological Monographs*, 1922, 31, No. 3, pp. 87.

19. McGEOCH, JOHN A., and WHITELY, PAUL L.: "The Recall of Observed Material," *Journal of Educational Psychology*, 1926, 17, 419–425.

20. MEUMANN, E.: *The Psychology of Learning: An Experimental Investigation of the Economy and Technique of Memory*, translated by John Wallace Baird. New York: D. Appleton [c. 1913], pp. xix, 393.

21. MITCHELL, ALICE MILLER: *Children and Movies*. Chicago: University of Chicago Press, 1929, pp. xxiv, 181.

22. MÜLLER, GEORG ELIAS: *Zur Analyse der Gedächtnistätigkeit und des Vorstellungsverlaufes*, 3 vols. Leipzig: J. A. Barth, 1911–1917.

23. MÜLLER, G. E., and SCHIEMANN, F.: *Experimentelle Beitrage zur Untersuchung des Gedächtnisse*. Hamburg: Voss, 1893.

24. PORTER, ELFA McWILLIAM: *The Curve of Retention in Moving Pictures for Young Children*. State University of Iowa, unpublished master's thesis, 1930, pp. 119.

25. RADOSSAWLJEWITSCH, P. R.: *Das Behalten und Vergessen bei Kindern und Erwachsenen nach Experimentellen Untersuchungen* (Das Fortschreiten des Vergessens mit der Zeit). Leipzig: Nemnich, 1907, pp. 197.

26. ROGERS, ROWLAND: "Cutting the Time of Learning," *Educational Screen*, 1925, 4, 13–14.

27. RUCH, G. M.: *The Objective or New-Type Examination: An Introduction to Educational Measurement*. Chicago: Scott, Foresman [c. 1929], pp. x, 478.

28. RUCH, G. M., and STODDARD, GEORGE D.: *Tests and Measurements in High School Instruction*. Yonkers-on-Hudson, N. Y.: World Book Co., 1927, pp. xix, 381.

29. SEABURY, WILLIAM MARSTON: *The Public and the Motion Picture Industry*. New York: Macmillan, 1926, pp. xiv, 340.

30. SEABURY, WILLIAM MARSTON: *Motion Picture Problems: The Cinema and the League of Nations.* New York: Avondale Press, 1929, pp. 426.
31. STARCH, DANIEL: *Educational Psychology.* New York: Macmillan, 1928, pp. ix, 568.
32. STECKER, H. DORA: "Children and the Moving Pictures: As Seen from the Box Office," *Child Welfare Magazine,* 1928–1929, 23, 59–62; 130–132.
33. THORNDIKE, EDWARD L.: *Educational Psychology. Vol. II: The Psychology of Learning.* New York: Teachers College, Columbia University [c. 1913], pp. xi, 452 (pp. 305–331).
34. WEBER, JOSEPH J.: "Bibliography on the Use of Visual Aids in Education," *Educational Screen,* 1930, 9, 29–31; 61–63; 93–95; 123–127; 155–159; 187–191.
35. WHITELY, PAUL L., and McGEOCH, JOHN A.: "The Curve of Retention for Poetry," *Journal of Educational Psychology,* 1928, 19, 471–479.
36. WILLIAMS, OSBORNE: "A Study of the Phenomenon of Reminiscence," *Journal of Experimental Psychology,* 1926, 9, 368–387.

INDEX

Action, classification of, 29, 53; retention of, 48, 79; types studied, 27, 53

Age-groups, 5; comparison of scores for, 45; methods of comparisons of, 46

Aims of study, 1

Analysis of pictures, preliminary steps, 2

Ballard, learning study by, 68

Boys, retention of, 59, 79

Child welfare, relation of present study to, 74

Comparison of children from different localities, 44

Completion test, type used, 7

Correlations, of picture content with test content, 27; of test results and themes, 26

Ebbinghaus, 67

Education, use of movies in, 74

Equation of observers, 10, 13

Essay, use of in testing, 17

Findings, effects of, 75; general, 31; utilization of, 73

General findings, 31

General information, effect of motion pictures on, 60; influence of reliability of, 62

General-information test, contents of, 3; divisions of, 3, 6

General test, directions for, 86; examples of, 86

Girls, retention of, 59, 79

Information for test items, reliability of, 60; requirements of, 60

Intelligence, comparison of for groups, 47

Jones, study by, 70

Measurement of retention, 41

Memory, formal technicalities of, 69; methods of testing, 67

Mental age, relation of to test scores, 33

Mitchell, study by, 71

Motion pictures, acceptance of contents of, 78; accuracy of contents of, 62; analysis of, 2; effects of on general information, 60, 77; experiments with, 70; list of, 7; retention of contents of, 78

Multiple-choice test, use of, 21

Observers, age-groups of, 5; age of, 13; intelligence quotients of, 13; mental age of, 13; number of, 2, 77; reading age of, 13; sampling of, 11

Oral test, material in, 30; procedure of, 30

Plot, retention of, 79

Preliminary picture analyses, 2

Purpose of study, 1

Relationships, between specific and general tests, 33; between test scores and ages, 33

Reliability of tests, 33

Retention, boys vs. girls, 59, 79; conditions affecting, 70; in children from different localities, 44; of action and background, 48; of incident, 54; of plot, 54; of specific information, 37; scores on, 42, 49

Retention of action and background, 48; variations in, 52

Retention of incident, compared with retention of plot, 54; factors influencing, 58; scores on, 56

Retention of plot, compared with retention of incident, 54; factors influencing, 58; scores on, 56

Retention of specific information,